Borderlines

The Edges of US Capitalism, Immigration, and Democracy

Borderlines

The Edges of US Capitalism, Immigration, and Democracy

Daniel Melo

Winchester, UK
Washington, USA

JOHN HUNT PUBLISHING

First published by Zero Books, 2021
Zero Books is an imprint of John Hunt Publishing Ltd., No. 3 East St., Alresford,
Hampshire SO24 9EE, UK
office@jhpbooks.com
www.johnhuntpublishing.com
www.zero-books.net

For distributor details and how to order please visit the 'Ordering' section on our website.

Text copyright: Daniel Melo 2020

ISBN: 978 1 78904 506 2
978 1 78904 507 9 (ebook)
Library of Congress Control Number: 2020938267

A CIP catalogue record for this book is available from the British Library.

Design: Stuart Davies

Printed and bound by CPI Group (UK) Ltd, Croydon, CR0 4YY
Printed in North America by CPI GPS partners

We operate a distinctive and ethical publishing philosophy in
all areas of our business, from our global network of authors to
production and worldwide distribution.

Contents

To the memory of all those lives destroyed by capitalism.
To the possibility of those we might yet save.

Acknowledgments

Special thanks to my parents and their immigration story. To my mother's feedback on drafts of the manuscript. To Professor Liccione for her assistance on this text and the imprint she has forever left on my writing. And to my wife, Krista, who continued to listen, talk through, and give insight about the text long after she should have been tired of hearing me ramble about it.

Chapter 1

An Introduction to Efficient Dehumanization

As we approached our office door, the sound of footsteps behind me went quiet. My colleague and I turned to see our client, Sara,[1] clutching her small son, silent tears emptying onto his dark black hair. But unlike so many of the parents, children, and tears that stream through immigration court, Sara had found safety. After grueling hours of testimony and a withering cross-examination, she won her asylum case.

A brutal cross-examination conducted, not by the government's prosecutor, but by *the judge*—looking for some slight inconsistency, some hint of implausibility, any reason, to deny her claim. She had suffered for years at the hands of a misogynist abuser in her home country, only to relive each moment of trauma in minute detail to have any hope of securing her escape. This is one of the cruel ironies of asylum law—the more exacting the circumstances were on one's humanity, the better chance at staying. At the end of his questioning, the judge remarked to the government's attorney that he could see no way around the case law and would *have* to grant Sara asylum, as though *he* had experienced some deep psychological torment.

Sara's tears in that hallway, just two elevator stops from where she fought for her life, stain the black robes of America's alleged democracy. The cruelty she experienced before fleeing her home country, the thousands of dangerous miles with her small child, none of it ended when she reached the US border. It simply donned a new face, one grinning with the joy of near impunity, drunk on the swill of indifference, and adorned with the crown of "constitutionality." She faced a new abuser—a system which did not recognize her as fully human. She had to wrench her and her son's humanity from the hands of that shifting evil, and at least for a day, succeeded. She was also among the last to do so on these grounds: about a year later, then-Attorney General Jeff Sessions tossed out the precedential Board of Immigration Appeals (BIA) case that recognized the right of women like Sara to asylum from persistent gender-based abuse by their partners.

This and the many other visible evils of the US immigration system prompt a very pertinent, humane, moral question — *Why?* Why is the system like this? Why would a judge cross-examine an abused woman for hours about her torment? Why would protection be here today and gone tomorrow?

To uncover the answers to these and a host of other questions about US immigration requires shifting the question itself. It is better asked as a question of *what. What* produced such an arbitrary, oppressive system? Approaching the system in this light reveals that its creation and sustenance lies in the material world. This *materialist* conception — how people engage with the world, organize themselves, and produce the things necessary to survive — looks for answers to social and political problems "not in men's brains, not in men's better insights into eternal truth and justice, but in changes in the modes of production and exchange."[2] In other words, the root cause of the oppression of migrants, the borderlines between people, Immigration and Customs Enforcement (ICE), immigration court, and even racism, must be explored within the context of the dominant economic system — capitalism. The politics surrounding immigration cannot be divorced from the economic realities that inform it.

It is impossible to understand or combat what Sara (or the many others like her) experienced without first understanding how migrants' identity has historically been tied to their ability to cheaply labor for the benefit of capitalism. Examining this reality and the forces that ensure migrant exploitation will call into question the fundamental self-proclaimed truths of equality, the rule of law, and the nature of democracy in America. It requires a look at not just the contours of the divisions between people—both migrant and citizen, worker and capitalist—but the powers and ideologies needed to protect those divisions. What makes migrants exploitable—their legal status—is the product of a necessarily oppressive system that attempts to control their bodies. The immigration system has not and will never work for the migrant. It *works* for the benefit and perpetuation of capitalism.

The first half of this book explores the historical material relationship between the US political-economic system, migration controls, and labor and how this interaction fostered and continues the growth of American capitalism. What emerges is a complex picture of how policy has been driven by the material realities confronting the state, citizens, and the migrants at their shores, and how each revolution of the system reinforces the status quo of class relationships and power. Whether it is legislative power or racial and xenophobic scapegoating and intra-class division, capitalism has successfully kept migrants as borderline humans and maintained control over their bodies. Sara and her son are two of many casualties of the commoditizing forces of capitalism.

The second half of the book transitions to the necessity of state power to perpetuate the economic and political system—one that is sovereign over both citizen and migrant. It explores how it is created and renewed and despite its abstract nature, is exercised in very real ways. Through examining different facets of the immigration system, the book reveals how this power is evident in borders, the criminalization of human movement, the myth of national security, and even the "rule of law." The long-standing brutality at the border exposes the reduction of human beings to nonpersons, unprotected life. The criminalization and detention of migrants pinpoints the deep inadequacy of due process, just as national security is leveraged to justify placing human beings outside the protections that citizens take for granted. Immigration court and its bureaucratic administrative counterparts evidence the deep gap between true justice and the complacent fantasy of it.

What is also exposed throughout is how thinly the line between citizen and migrant is drawn, how close the evils that impact so many migrant lives are not far from all others. The nature of sovereign power, much like the economic system that nourishes it, has an innate control of its citizens and is not accountable to them. As this reality unfolds, it becomes clear why attempts at "better" humanitarian treatment of migrants fall flat. They are premised on the myth of a national commitment to universal ideals of justice and equality. Foreign policy, economic considerations, and personal ideology have always guided the application of humanitarian benefits like family reunification and even asylum and refugee policy. Through their exclusion from the full rights of citizenship (except through incredibly narrow and arbitrary processes), migrants reveal the brokenness of the very concepts of justice and democracy in America, and with it, the fragility of citizenship itself. The law, from the frail Constitution down to the jagged edges of shifting agency regulations and internal policy, merely memorializes the nation-state's monopoly over immigrant bodies and the very citizenry that it is supposed to serve.

Thus, the *what* question is predicated on the ongoing balancing act within capitalism of the need of cheap labor, dealing with the ire of the citizen working class, weighed against broader capitalist and empire-building goals on the international stage. The *what* is how the wage-labor relationship (and exploitation thereof) is part of the same conditions that give rise to Sara's nightmare and those of so many others. The *what* question reveals a cycle of exploitation that requires power and power that requires the resources to maintain itself. The *what* that stands on the borderline between migrant and citizen is an economic system that seeks to perpetuate itself at the expense of both.

The book wraps up by rejecting the broken approaches to migration reform and the failure of neo-liberalism to fix the present system. On the one hand, any attempt to humanize migrants independent of addressing the economic system that continues to commodify them is ultimately insufficient. Without breaking the capitalist hold on labor, there is no law, no matter how carefully crafted, that will not result in manifest injustice towards the migrant. On the other, attempting to address the monstrosity of capitalism without global solidarity across borders is equally fraught, as the US's power to control migrant bodies within its territory is nearly unequivocal.

The remedy to the *what* question requires a radical rethinking of democracy and justice, both economic and political. An inalienable presumption of humanity and an accompanying right of each individual to demand and give an accounting for their treatment. This envisions more than open borders or legalization of migrants, but a union of working classes across boundaries towards a mutually justifiable future free of the dominating and exploitative nature of capitalism. Despite the power that capitalism holds over the stuff of life, the conclusions drawn here are neither deterministic nor pessimistic in their outlook. The demand for justification from the political and economic powers, together with an embrace of a robust ideal of democracy, are rooted in a deep optimism that the barriers towards true equality and freedom can be seen and removed.

If we return to that hallway, Sara's tears, and her son's embrace, there is more present than the evils of the system. Despite the crushing weight of the legalities stacked against her, she prevailed. The system, for all of its power and injustice, was built by human hands, and can be torn down by them. The working class is capable of seizing American democracy, despite its deeply flawed trajectory, with the aim of correcting it away from domination, exploitation, and dehumanization. Immigrants like Sara hold a mirror up to America, reminding its

people that the alleged promise of rest and safety for the tired—
even if those in power had no intention of keeping it—is one all
can make to themselves. The fight for migrant liberation is also
one for liberation of self.

Chapter 2

Legislating Human Commodities

This chapter explores key points in the US's immigration history and policy and how it emerged through the relationship between immigrants, capitalism, and state power. While there are competing, sometimes contradictory, forces at work, the pervasive need for cheap labor within the capitalist system largely dictates the need for control over immigrant rights and immigration flows.[1] Even outside of direct labor issues, the remaining legislative moves are products of other material realities produced within capitalism. In the end both are part of the ongoing balancing act between exploitation and exclusion, which are often only facially at odds. Both serve one another to ensure migrants remain vulnerable and that the status quo continues.

Articles of Commerce

Immigration law is a product of class relations. It exists, as legal scholar Mary Bilder argues, in "the shadow of slaves and indentured servants."[2] Long before the nation's independence, the indentured servitude trade dominated the immigrant landscape in the American colonies (though the servants had yet to actually be termed immigrants). From 1650 to 1780 an estimated 600,000 Europeans migrated to the colonies, most of which were "imported white servants," providing a much-needed cheap labor force in the colonies.[3] Apart from helping expand the economy directly, the human trade itself was profitable—merchants received payment from the British government to ship convicts to the colonies or payment from the colonies for the sale of convicts and other indentured servants.[4] Bilder writes: "For England's commercial culture, indentured servants were just one more article of commerce."[5] Migrants were commodities. While early migrants were never treated like slaves, they were commoditized in a similar fashion.

Early colonial laws focused on trying to prevent convicts from disrupting local life or relieving communities of the responsibility to care for impoverished or sick servants who were unable to work.[6] These early attempts at restriction evidence an underlying reality guiding migration policy—the contribution to the economic system is paramount over and often at the expense of humanitarian problems.[7]

As the slave trade grew, there was a shift in the perception of immigrants, as white European migrants were repulsed at the idea that colonial society categorized them as legally equivalent to black slaves.[8] While race was still an emerging concept, this increasingly racialized division between imported servants and slaves would lead to a legal tension—in order for the recently established federal government to regulate both, it had to consider both "articles of commerce."[9] As Bilder notes—"It was rapidly becoming impossible to maintain both that all people were 'articles of commerce' and to continue to uphold [local] state power to exclude certain people."[10] Either all incoming people were essentially property, white servant and black slave alike, or they were people, outside of federal power and left to each state to decide.

While this question was never fully resolved in the Supreme Court, due in part to the freeing of slaves (and rendering the distinction between servants and slaves moot), the concept of immigrants as "articles of commerce" was eventually rolled up into their regulation as incident to sovereignty.[11] The tensions between indentured servitude and slavery as well as the early restrictions on migrants in early America reveal something other than a pursuit of "universal human rights" that justified power over these bodies—"the explanation for legal doctrine often lies, not in a faith in enduring principles or a quest for or original meaning, but in the twisted history of legal assumptions, cultural perceptions, and social strife."[12]

Despite these early tensions over who had exclusive control of migrant bodies, less than a decade after the end of the Revolutionary War, Congress passed the Naturalization Act of 1790. This act allowed a "free white person" to naturalize as a citizen. Early legislation required swearing fealty to the US, high physical presence durations, and the still-standing requirement that a person be of "good moral character." These exclusionary approaches were in part racial and also to prevent too many outsiders (like the growing masses of the Irish working-poor) from subverting America with a revolution of their own.[13] A 1795 act gave the president a nearly unchecked and disturbing power—the ability to detain or cast out any immigrant in the name of national security. The self-preservation of elite class interests is evident even in early "humanitarian" relief efforts as well. In 1803, Congress enacted a seemingly significant reform— banning the "importation of any negro, mulatto, or other person of colour," signaling the end of the US-international slave trade (slavery itself did not end for over another half-century). But this reform was ultimately a protection against the Haitian immigrant. White plantation owners feared Haitian migrants could lead a revolt in the south after the Haitian revolution expelled its colonizers.[14] Immigration restrictions in America's early democracy were in the interests of the preservation of power.

Meanwhile, on the US southern border, the Treaty of Guadalupe Hidalgo handed over vast swaths of Mexico to the US and purportedly allowed Mexican property owners to retain their land rights as if they were citizens of the US. This was very different from reality—as Mexican American land claims arose under the treaty, the US government and judiciary consistently denied them, rendering it a hollow promise to these annexed immigrants.[15]

Reconstruction to the Great Depression

During Reconstruction and the sudden unavailability of slaves, the nation was in desperate need of inexpensive labor. In a bid to recruit workers, President Lincoln signed the 1864 "Act to Encourage Immigration" which centralized immigration authority with the federal government but also made contracts for labor enforceable in the US—"whereby emigrants shall pledge the wages of their labor for a term not exceeding twelve months to repay the expenses of their emigration"— in essence a re-legalization of indentured servitude. Even when laborers freed themselves, the aforementioned deepening divide of "white" versus "other" migrants or slaves emerged to further oppress the later categories.

Before the end of the nineteenth century, Congress extinguished the last light of any sort of "open" border and with it, consolidated its power over immigration. While the Page Act of 1875 tried to end legal indentured servitude and trafficking of Asian laborers and women, it also came with the very first restrictive language around a person's character. These echoed earlier colonial laws that banned convicted felons (other than political crimes) from entry into the US (who were perceived as poor workers). The gates to America shut even tighter in 1882 as Congress passed the Chinese Exclusion Act, banning all Chinese peoples from immigrating for 10 years and permitted the deportation of any "unauthorized" Chinese migrants. Those allowed to remain were barred from naturalization, cutting them off from any political protection and guaranteeing tighter control over the flow of labor into the country. This move is exemplary of a reality that repeats itself—capitalism will deliver as few rights as possible for the maximal benefit to itself.

By the end of the nineteenth century, Congress had expanded the list of exclusions (and deportable offenses) for immigrants with contagious diseases, "idiots," insane persons, paupers, anyone who could become a public charge on society, people who had committed a "crime of moral turpitude," and anarchists—all with readily identifiable problems as it pertained to questions of labor and political power. This era also saw the beginnings of the enforcement arm of the state to regulate America's borders and coasts.

Federal control over labor flows featured prominently in early twentieth century legislation, with the first law establishing numerical quotas. At the time, it was equal to 3 percent of the foreign-born population of that nationality in the 1910 census (most Asian countries were still barred altogether).[16] This coincided with the early century's high nationalist fervor together with growing fears of foreign leftists and anarchists, an ethno-nationalist hope of stemming the tide of political refugees fleeing Europe and their potential to disrupt capitalism's ideological grip.[17]

While the nation was focused there, Latinx migration surged with minimal legislative restriction. Not that their entrance was welcomed and pain-free. Many Mexicans that entered the US at a port of entry had to pay a costly registration fee, subject themselves to "cleanings" in the form of kerosene baths and fumigation with Zyklon B,[18] while others, understandably, simply crossed at unofficial places, as they had done for decades, to avoid these evils.

The southern border increasingly show-cased the competing interests within capitalism between capitalists, migrants, and the citizen working class, mixed in with the growing power of race that had gathered steam from the previous century. Congress had looked to reduce the number of Mexican workers entering the country on several occasions, but repeatedly, southwestern employers fiercely objected. Not out of the kindness of their hearts—the agribusinesses lobby, one heavily dependent on migrant labor, successfully defeated these measures on the promise that the Mexican was not an "immigrant" but more like "a pigeon [who] goes back to roost."[19] Most agribusiness employers readily agreed with many whites-only nativists that Mexicans were racially unfit to be US citizens.[20] However, the southwestern employers had a critical need for these "lesser" people's labor, again tying the exploitability of migrants to their lawful place in society.[21] As the conflict steadily grew between the capitalist need for labor and the xenophobic fears that had arisen elsewhere (all under the looming pressure-cooker of the Great Depression), an alarming compromise took place.

Senator Coleman Blease, a white supremacist from South Carolina, introduced a bill that would make unlawful entry a misdemeanor, and a return entry after deportation a felony. This measure, rather than an aggressive restriction on the border, allowed the nativists to target migrants in the country while agriculture could continue to employ migrants with the added benefit of holding incarceration over their heads. This bill sailed through Congress.

The criminalization of immigrants also brought the beginnings of the prison-industrial complex. The US prosecuted and imprisoned tens of thousands of Mexicans (sometimes making up 99 percent of jailed immigrants during the law's early years).[22] The government did not enforce it along strictly legal vs. illegal lines but used it to target Mexicans broadly. Approximately 1.2 million of the estimated 2 million people the US forcibly removed to Mexico were American citizens.[23] Here, the separation between migrant flows and rights can be seen keenly. Business interests needed inexpensive labor and so long as that was not wholly disrupted, they gladly acquiesced to what Professor Kelly Lytle Hernandez notes was a eugenicist bid to erase the Mexican (lawful citizen or not) laborer from the American identity.[24]

The path first blazed by the colonial perception of immigrants as commerce had come full circle to be both cause and effect— capitalists benefited from a commoditized population kept under the thumbby racialized, legal distinctions but also justified and continued that oppression because migrants fell outside of political protection as something less than people.

WWII and Onward

WWII demanded another shift in policy, but once again, not based on egalitarian principles. In 1942, due to massive labor shortages, Congress worked with the Mexican government to create the Bracero Program.[25] Bracero permitted Mexican men, without their families, to enter the US for short-term, mostly agricultural, labor contracts. The millions of braceros[26] fueled capitalist expansion and the military-industrial complex.[27]

Not that the braceros were considered patriots or heroes — they suffered at the hands of business and the authorities alike. The state of Idaho approved rules forcing braceros to stay at their assigned jobs or face arrest (and then be forced to labor while awaiting trial).[28] Elsewhere, agricultural employers subjected braceros to malnourishment, unfair pay, and substandard housing and yet were assured protection by local law enforcement and immigration officials who would round up and forcibly return escaping migrants.[29] The use of state power became increasingly more explicit as a means of preserving the dehumanizing relationships that propelled the nation forward economically.

WWII also produced one of the nation's boldest justifications for subhuman treatment of migrants and their families. In 1942, President Roosevelt signed Executive Order 9066, authorizing the incarceration of Japanese Americans living within 100 miles of the coast as a "wartime measure." This included freezing their bank accounts, forcing them to leave their homes and businesses, and the incarceration of nearly 122,000 men, women, and children.[30] Two-thirds were US citizens.[31] Order 9066 did not go unchallenged, and *Korematsu v. US* laid bare how little the commoditized view of immigrants had changed. Fred Korematsu was tried and convicted for violating the curfew portion of Order

9066. The Supreme Court upheld his conviction and the order's constitutionality on the principle of military necessity,[32] the exercise of unquestionable sovereignty (in this case, delegated to a single person) over the population, citizens or not.

The mid-twentieth century saw Congress pass the Immigration and Nationality Act (INA) in 1965, which set forth many of the modern governing principles of immigration law and narrow paths towards legal status. This was in addition to numerous other laws, some of which improved migrant treatment—finally allowing migrants from certain Asian countries to naturalize; allowing refugee admissions; visas for family reunification; skilled worker migration; and the Cuban Adjustment Act. The high court even handed down a pro-migrant decision in *Plyler v. Doe*, allowing undocumented children into public schools.

Yet, these shifts cannot be divorced from issues of class and labor. "Operation Wetback" targeted undocumented Mexicans even as the Bracero Program was in full swing. Despite its celebrated nature, the court in *Plyler* was largely sympathetic to a child's lack of agency within the immigration system, but was fine with the idea of Texas passing labor laws to prohibit undocumented employment.[33] As explored more fully later in the book, asylum and refuge were and continued to be dictated by foreign policy and economic considerations.

Even Reagan's 1986 (in)famous amnesty was first sold as a crackdown—it opened the door of status to nearly 3 million people but left out 2 million more and increased immigration enforcement spending to secure the border.[34] Measures that improve the circumstances for some migrants have rarely been pursued on exclusively universalist principles of humanitarian treatment and are often packaged with increased enforcement. Legal immigration creates narrow channels that can be easily turned-off while ensuring that enforcement and other targeted measures prevent migrants from readily organizing or establishing any other foothold within the system.

The end of the twentieth century also saw the passage of further restrictions with the Illegal Immigration Reform and Immigrant Responsibility Act (IIRAIRA) under Clinton that finished putting the cogs in place for the egregious deportation machine present today. IIRAIRA, as its title suggests, was far from a pro-migrant reform—it made many people deportable while burning the bridge for others to obtain status. It made a number of non-violent offenses deportable crimes (even for green card holders) and made them retroactive. It created the due process nightmare of "expedited removal" wherein low-level immigration officers can remove anyone apprehended within 100 miles of the border and mandated immigrant detention before removing them. It raised an incredibly high bar for anyone seeking cancellation of removal (protection against deportation) by requiring them to show hardship to a US citizen child or spouse (and 10 years' presence) regardless of the immigrant's personal circumstances. It blocked undocumented migrants from applying for status directly in the US if they had someone who could petition for them and created 3- and 10-year bans to re-entry for those that left. In essence, it re-instituted the deportation campaigns of the Great Depression Era, and together with the INA and subsequent regulations, hopelessly complicated the system. This complexity is now a feature, rather than a bug, and helps continue the exploitative power of the system into the modern era.

The final brief stop in the US legislation of immigrants is Congress's passing of the PATRIOT Act in 2002 after 9/11. The Act completely renovated immigration enforcement mechanisms by creating the Department of Homeland Security whose faces now include ICE, the United States Citizenship and Immigration Service, and Border Patrol (CBP). It charted new territory in increasingly militarized border and "police" forces. It reinforced the Attorney General's power to jail any immigrant he or she reasonably believes threatens national security (regardless of what immigration relief is available). It, together with subsequent amendments, fundamentally deepened the state's ability to justify its broad actions in the enduring language of national security, throwing such a wide net that, to quote the BIA, "is breathtaking in its scope."[35]

Despite many of these consistently loathsome legislative approaches to migrants, there is no grand, organized capitalist conspiracy to keep migrants under the thumb. There were instances of improving migrant conditions and attempts to bring them closer to personhood that, at least facially, seem to bring migrants out of their commoditized, nonperson past. However, to attempt to view each turn of the immigration machine as one that is either "good" or "bad" is to accept a false dichotomy and merely perpetuates the myth of a fair system. It is to argue, as far too many have, that migrants only deserve better, more humane treatment, something a bit less arbitrary.

What is truly required is an understanding of how an economic system can create and justify treatment of people as less than people. Even if the nation's choices about immigrants exist along a spectrum from malice on one end to well-intended (albeit at times, ignorant) benevolence on the other, both arise from and return to questions of power, politics, and money. In order to reach a truly just outcome for citizens and migrants alike, the very heart of the social, economic, and political order must be exposed in all of its divisive, dangerous, and exploitative strength. While this chapter noted a few instances, the next chapter examines the material origins and the role of the ideologies of race, xenophobia, and how they shaped American democracy and migrant treatment.

Chapter 3

Race, Xenophobia, and Democracy

In the wake of Trump's election, xenophobia and race have reappeared with a virulence that many considered part of a bygone era. Yet, as shown in the previous chapter, they have been present and woven throughout the tug of war over migrant bodies. Trump's "bad hombres" rhetoric, the populace's demand to protect American jobs, secure the border, or preserve the American identity and way of life are a series of old adages with new paint. Given their reappearance, it would be easy to conclude that xenophobia and racism are at the heart of the gap between migrants and citizens; that they are simply part of the broader cultural debate about what America "is."

However, in the same moment, there appears to be a post-racial approach to immigration policy. There are an estimated 50,000 undocumented Irish immigrants in the US,[1] most of them visa overstays. While this number is much smaller than the number of undocumented immigrants from Mexico, they are a large enough group to gain notice and sympathy back home and even tried to plead their case to Trump post-election.[2] They were also the subject of a hypothetical question from former Fox News Anchor Bill O'Reilly to then-presidential candidate Ted Cruz during the 2016 election cycle. O'Reilly asked Cruz whether he would deport a fictional Irishman — "So Tommy O'Malley from Co Cork in Ireland is over here and he overstays his visa and he has got a couple of kids and he has settled into Long Island, and you, President Cruz, are going to send the Feds to his house, take him out and put him on a plane back to Ireland?" Cruz (who, like an estimated 34.5 million Americans, has Irish heritage) responds — "You Better believe it."[3] Cruz's approach came to pass. Since Trump's election, ICE has detained and deported increasing numbers of undocumented Irish, as Boston's ICE office commented, "ICE is apprehending all those in violation of immigration laws regardless of national origin."[4]

Thus, on the one hand, race and xenophobia appear to continue their central part in informing immigration policy, while on the other, are stripped entirely from it. This contradiction cannot be resolved on its face and instead requires a deeper look into the material conditions that birthed the constructs of race and xenophobia. Despite occasionally producing inconsistent approaches and policy, race and xenophobia's roles in American democracy and working-class animosity have consistently helped perpetuate the class structure.

The constructs of race and xenophobia

Race is a relatively recent phenomenon. As Kenan Malik argues in his books *The Meaning of Race*[5] and *Strange Fruit*[6]—the beginning of racial categorization and its evolution had far less to do with superficial physical features than it did socio-cultural factors. Malik points out that, scientifically, race is non-existent—there are no "pure" races.[7] Most genetic variation occurs within races and homo sapiens are far too young a species for racial variation to embed itself in evolutionary biology.[8] Rather, racial categories were the product of a conflict between Enlightenment ideals of human equality and the obvious material inequality that persisted amongst the classes.[9] Out of that conflict, Malik argues, race emerged—the difference between classes was fixed because of some hereditary, biological cause.[10] Race is not a biological reality, but a product of the class antagonism and inequality. It is a historical entity, a social construction created through human interaction.[11]

While xenophobia, "the fear or hatred of strangers or foreigners," is a modern term from the nineteenth century,[12] it has older material origins. Biologists believe this fear is rooted in two evolved human instincts—territoriality and the endowment effect.[13]

Territoriality dictates that an individual or group with control over resources sees those resources as scarce and will seek to protect them against outsiders.[14] As Professor Steven Neuberg notes, it is not just a question of resource competition but a question of social organization and survival—"Foreigners with different rules might interfere with the social coordination you need to do important tasks, or might get members of your group to follow their rules instead."[15]

The endowment effect centers on how ownership creates such a high subjective value that it is difficult to divorce the owner of the object or belief.[16] This effect inclines people to reject values outside of the ones they possess.[17] Thus, even during prosperous economic times, xenophobia still surfaces to protect a particular culture, set of values, and a particular group's dominance in social and political life. While a great deal more could be said about both, the key element here is xenophobia's material nature—not forever encoded in human nature, but socially constructed.

Forgoing a lengthy discussion of race's entire development (and xenophobia's use) in colonial and post-revolution America, there is a strong example of its constructed nature within early Irish immigration. Periods of discrimination against Irish, Celts, Slavs, and Jews, in the late nineteenth and early twentieth century, evidence how the boundary lines for "white" shifted over time. As Professor Natalia Molina writes in *How Race is Made in America*, "White was not a monolithic category but a hierarchical one, with shades of whiteness."[18] Xenophobia worked against these outsiders (be they Catholic, Jewish, Polish, etc.) despite a shared skin color, as some groups attempted to preserve the "American" way of life.

In order for Irish immigrants to gain some measure of security and not be seen as a threat, the goalposts for race had to move. The lesser shades of white, like the Irish, obtained acceptance into the middle and upper social classes by defining themselves as what they were *not*: brown and black.[19] As discussed in the previous chapter, this push to identify with the class in power (in the hope of a better life) helped lay down the border of race. As further evidence of this constructed divide, in the same period, Mexicans who did possess land and money were able to access some of the privileges associated with whiteness.[20] However, as land was taken from so many of them after Guadalupe Hidalgo (and with it, the vestiges of political power), the color of one's skin became an increasingly strong divisor, and in the case of Mexicans in the US, cemented their place as an inferior people.[21] The construct of race not only served as a means of certain working-class migrants like the Irish to elevate their status; it also helped justify terrible treatment of low-wage brown migrants by denying them any political protection or basic rights.[22]

This is but one example of the emergence of race and racialized thinking over time in America and how the material world cemented racial categorization within two different migrant populations. But it also raises questions: How do the dividing lines of race and xenophobia help perpetuate the class structure? Aren't the ideas of racial immigration exclusion and capitalist labor needs at odds? Shouldn't democracy protect against their use in policy? Despite the US holding itself out as a model democracy, what emerges from the historical record is not only racial and xenophobic thinking in immigration policy, but also how it has worked in service of both money and power.[23]

Tools for the powerful

In their study of race in immigration policy, scholars Fitzgerald and Cook-Martin note how capitalists routinely leveraged ethnic discrimination and xenophobia to their benefit.[24] At times, despite strong racist and xenophobic sentiments among the population, higher considerations of the nation-state like diplomacy or business interests carried the day.[25] For example, parts of Latin

America and the Philippines had periods of exemption from immigration restriction because of US commercial and military connections, even though most US citizens viewed them as inferior peoples.[26] Even during the Trump era, the use of an explicitly racialized and xenophobic policy like the "Muslim Ban" does not include Muslim-majority countries where the Trump Organization has done business or pursued potential deals.[27]

The contradictions of racialized logic can make for strange bedfellows—labor unions could be convinced to side with the capitalists against migrants.[28] For their part, the capitalists had no need of legitimating immigrants and saw no contradiction between racist ideology and commerce, as Fitzgerald notes during the nineteenth century—"Business interests wanted a reserve labor army of cheap Chinese labor, not Chinese neighbors or fellow citizens."[29]

This blend of material interests and ideologies explains why Mexicans were not included in the racial quota acts of the early twentieth century, even though they were very low on the racial hierarchy.[30] Here's southern Democrat John Box in 1928—"The Mexican peons are illiterate and ignorant. Because of their unsanitary habits and living conditions and their vices they are especially subject to smallpox, venereal diseases, tuberculosis, and other dangerous contagions...Few, if any, other immigrants have brought us so large a proportion of criminals and paupers as the Mexican peons."[31] What protected them from racial exclusion was not equality or democracy but the idea that they were "birds of passage," which convinced policy-makers that they would return to Mexico when employment demand slackened and not threaten the racial makeup of the country.[32]

Even with the superseding interests of capital and foreign policy, race found a way to scapegoat and eventually help police migrant bodies all the same. As noted in the previous chapter, Blease's criminalization of migrants contorted migration into a moral issue (which continues into the present)—unlawful entrants were lawbreakers, reinforcing the notion of the migrants as criminals and inferior people. This, in turn, justified the system's oppression and exploitation of them and yet did not run afoul of labor needs, as it solidified the capitalist stranglehold on labor flow.

Race even shaped the contours of the protections of citizenship and provided the means to abridge them. Seventy percent of the detained Japanese were US citizens during WWII,[33] contrasted with Germans and Italians who the state primarily detained on the basis of their alienage. Angelo Rossi, the second-generation Italian mayor of San Francisco in 1942, testified before a Congressional Committee that he believed that internment would cause a great deal of suffering; but his concern was only for German and Italian Americans whose "problems should be considered separately from those of the Japanese."[34] Mayor Rossi, as did much of the nation, considered the American German and Italians to be sufficiently like them, so as not to pose a threat. But even this approach was never far removed from economic reality. Where business was paramount, the Japanese had an importance that superseded their otherness—they were crucial to the economic health of Hawaii and the state detained far fewer of them.[35]

Race and xenophobia's ongoing virulence

In the present, it should be no surprise that these constructs hold, even amongst those that should most readily look beyond race and seek solidarity with other migrants. As Irish journalist and critic Fintan O'Toole notes about the Irish attitudes towards Latinx people—"The 50,000 or so 'undocumented Irish' in the US are human beings. They work hard. They contribute to the economy and society...They are Us. But all those other millions of shadow people? They are Them. At best, they are anonymous, interchangeable figures...At worst, they are 'bad hombres.'"[36]

As is evident in the case of the undocumented Irish, the racial gap between them and the undocumented Latinx is a rehashing of the same approach the Irish took over a century ago—by defining themselves as what they are *not*. They seek acceptance into the political and social order by casting others downward, reducing Latinx people as something less than human in an effort to secure their own protection and stability within a broken and exploitative system. The reiteration of this approach points to the necessity of inverting the way one thinks about race, immigration, and democracy. Race and xenophobia did not produce the dividing lines between migrant populations or them and citizens. Rather, these borders appeared in response to material needs—a way of explaining and justifying class divisions, of gaining acceptance for those who once weren't "white," of breeding division where there should be solidarity.

Even the institution of liberal democracy can and has been leveraged to exclude peoples who were not considered suitable for self-government and therefore should have no say in US democratic institutions.[37] Despite the facial "de-racialization" of modern immigration enforcement and the overall trend of decreasing obviously discriminatory policies, race continues to play a role in migration policy and American democracy.[38] This should be unsurprising. As Fitzgerald points out—"Racial egalitarianism is not inherently sustained by liberalism."[39] There is nothing within the present US democratic framework that prevents explicitly racializing migration. The courts have long recognized the state's unchecked power to regulate immigration, even on a racial basis.[40]

In all instances—whether the business interests, the racialized thinking that they and the economic system perpetuated amongst the working class, or other foreign policy considerations that drive migrant treatment—the material conditions of capitalism developed and ensured that race and xenophobia emerged as a means of divesting both yesterday's and today's migrant of personhood. Despite their chaotic and at times contradictory nature, race and xenophobia can be bent in service of perpetuating the status quo.

Even with their ubiquity and persistence, the fact that these divisions were constructed in the first place is also their weakness—they can be demolished by human hands and on those ruins, something new and better can be built. People are capable of seeing through the fog.

Molina notes in mid-twentieth century California, people of color who were protesting immigrant detainment facilities recognized a shared oppression—"Wonder if those cops realize how it makes us Negro people feel when they start kicking the Mexicans around?"[41] This oppression was connected in numerous ways, recognized by activists—then-Attorney General Herbert Brownell's (at the time, the Department of Justice oversaw immigration enforcement) refusal to investigate the murder of 14-year-old Emmett Till.[42] Or the "black codes" used to continue to exploit black labor after the Civil War which were alarmingly similar to the methods used to keep migrant laborers under the boot of abusive agriculturalists.[43]

Throughout the book, the links between migrant, citizen, and a broken democracy will become more visible. Economic and political justice are deeply intertwined. The struggle for humanizing migrants, the eradication of racism and xenophobia, and breaking free of capitalism are connected not just by necessity, but, more significantly, by their possibility. A possibility for a new kind of being that has cast off the chains of an exploitative economic system and the attendant evils of hate over skin color or perceived cultural inferiority. The end of racism and xenophobia requires a radical rethinking of economic and political organization and what it means to be a person within it.

Chapter 4

The Modern Face of Labor Exploitation

The question of labor has always been at the heart of America's relationship and presumed control over immigrants. This chapter focuses down to the present dynamic of labor and migration in the US and how it reveals one of the contradictions within capitalism—the worker is simultaneously a unique source of value for production and profit (all as cheaply as possible), and yet, indispensable as a consumer who increasingly lacks the means of obtaining the very things she produces.[1] This contradiction of unrestricted economic development and accumulation of wealth for their own sakes' finds a direct contradiction in its inability to realize perpetual profit because it lacks consumers.[2]

Migrant labor has long served as a buffer when capitalism is confronted with this contradiction and the accompanying decrease in profit, forming part of what Marx termed the necessary "reserve army of labor."[3] By exploiting readily available migrant bodies, capitalism continues its attempt at a balancing act to maximize its gains without having to confront the human consequences of reducing people to the bare minimum of living. This chapter explores how cheap migrant labor (documented and undocumented) and citizens' own conscription into the reserve army of labor continue to preserve profit for the few.

Capitalism's need for undocumented laborers

As they have for generations, migrants continue to occupy a significant share of the "low-skill" labor jobs that still exist in the US, particularly given how few they are compared to the greater population. The Pew Research Center estimates that undocumented migrants accounted for 26 percent of all farming jobs, 15 percent of all construction, nine percent of all production jobs and 9 percent of service jobs, despite being only 5 percent of the overall workforce.[4] The conservative, "low-immigration, pro-immigrant" Federation for American Immigration Reform (FAIR) found that "the farming sector has grown increasingly dependent on a steady supply of workers who have entered the country illegally..." and yet, "the agribusiness sector has consistently opposed an immigration policy that would result in a legal workforce."[5]

FAIR's position is that current hiring practices are crucial for the survival of the industry, as Americans are not willing to do agricultural work and increasing wages to attract native-born workers would result in significantly higher food prices or a decline in American food production."[6] The report also acknowledges "Federal authorities have long turned a blind eye to the rampant use of illegal workers..."[7]

While FAIR's complaint has far more to do with the wage-suppressing effect that migrant labor exploitation has on American workers (and thus ignores the actual culprit—the system that requires their exploitation), it does get something right: agriculture profits have grown on the backs of undocumented labor. To reverse this long-standing tendency would require significant wage increases (40 percent or more)[8] to replace undocumented workers. This reality also applies to the construction and service sectors as well—migrant labor has long helped prop-up the industry.[9]

The system necessarily ties exploitation to the very means of survival for everyday people in the form of cheap commodities. As the demand for decent food has increased, so too has the need for US farmers to compete in a global capitalist economy. According to a study done by the Partnership for a New American Economy (PNAE), from 1998 to 2012, US consumption of imported produce rose by nearly 79 percent.[10] The labor-profit contradiction of capitalism dictates that workers have to stretch their low wages to seek out cheaper homes, hotel rooms, restaurant meals, and milk and that these demands fuel the reduction of labor costs that commoditize migrants. Because capitalists cannot push wages much lower lest consumption fall off altogether, profit margins must be amplified and protected by some other means—cheap migrant labor.

Despite this, there is still more profit to be wrung from agriculture's tree. PNAE notes there was as much as $3.3 billion in missed GDP growth in 2012 alone because of labor shortages.[11] This labor shortage comes even as there are unlimited visas available for temporary agricultural workers, which has nevertheless failed to reduce undocumented workers.[12]

This raises a significant question: How can the US be exploiting migrant labor when there is a "shortage" of them? Should that not drive wages up? The 2008 economic crash explains much of this dichotomy. The current labor gap and the industry's inability to fill spaces with American workers return back to the contradiction within capitalism of labor as a cost to be reduced. While the Great Recession has driven down the available labor pool, it has done so largely in the context of undocumented workers, specifically, young men.[13] As the conservative think tank Center for Immigration Studies notes—when the agricultural and construction industries complain of labor shortages, what they mean is that the easily exploited labor pool has dried up and they face the possibility of having to raise wages.[14]

Shortage or not, undocumented immigrants stand little chance of improving conditions for themselves through collective action. Labor exploitation and poverty wages need power to sustain themselves, thus linking legal status to labor. As has long been the case, the lack of status provides employers with a legal whip to keep migrants in their place. Business can leverage state power in the form of ICE and the threat of incarceration and deportation should workers demand more humane conditions (or in some cases, payment at all).[15]

Capitalism's control over undocumented migrant bodies through the immigration system ensures that low-skilled labor remains as cheap as possible and continues the tradition of commoditizing migrants. They are easily replaced and unable to raise their voice against their oppressors. Because profitability and unemployment are so closely tied together in the system, capitalist protection of profit at the expense of jobs during the Great Recession has actually driven down the number of migrants looking for work. If history is any indication, this will inevitably require a new balancing of immigrant rights and labor flows, but assuredly with minimal, if any, gains in the former to achieve needs in the latter.

Skilled labor too

Legal labor immigration has many of the same problems. The exemplary of exploitation in this context is the H-1B non-immigrant visa, which in the recent decade has primarily been used to import labor for science, tech, engineering, and math (STEM) fields.[16] The H-1B program allows employers to fill positions that require specialized knowledge or skills with foreign workers, so long as they can show that the US workforce cannot meet those needs. The visa confers non-immigrant status, which is under a strict time limit and only allows the migrant to work in the same field she obtained a visa for.

Employers, albeit subtly, are using H-1B laborers to reduce labor costs. For much of the last decade, numerous STEM industries have claimed labor shortages, with some estimates claiming up to 3 million job openings as of 2017.[17] While there is disagreement amongst the experts and academics studying the H-1B market whether there is an actual shortage or it is occupation and locality specific, what is clear—STEM companies recognize how to use immigrants to protect profits.

Despite laying off over 7700 employees in 2015, Microsoft had asserted back in a 2012 report that it was facing a significant shortage of labor and that the H-1B program should be expanded.[18] This layoff came even as Microsoft upped its H-1B applications in 2015 from 2014 to over 4500.[19] The details betray the cost-saving effect of using migrant labor. Daniel Costa noted in his 2012 paper on Microsoft's claims that the unemployment rate in STEM fields for college-educated workers, which normally ranged around 1.2 to 1.7 percent, jumped to 3.4 post-recession.[20] Costa also points out that from 2000 to 2011, computer and math laborers wages had increased less than two dollars, further undermining the notion of a true labor shortage.[21] Here, as was the case with undocumented workers, the shortage is one of exploitable, cost-reducing migrants.

The reality of this exploitation is further evident in the actual wages paid to H-1B immigrants. Part of the immigration process facially attempts to mitigate labor abuses by requiring employers to certify to the government that they will pay the migrant a wage equal or more than the prevailing wage paid to other workers. However, as Professor Ron Hira noted in his testimony before a Congressional Subcommittee concerning employer abuse of H-1B visas, the Department of Labor (DOL) gives companies enormous deference on how the prevailing wage is determined based on occupation and skill level.[22] Hira also testified that employers "routinely select the lowest skill levels and pad their profits by hiring H-1Bs at the lowest possible 'prevailing wage' levels.[23] In Fiscal Year 2015, 41 percent of the workers approved by the government were at wage Level 1...Level 1 wages are typically 40 percent below the average wage."[24] He goes on to testify that the DOL approved nearly four out of five applications at the two lowest wage levels.[25]

Hira also testified that employers gain discounts on more than salary and the system ensures their ability to protect those gains. Firing the immigrant worker terminates the visa, making it almost impossible to organize the workers or blow the whistle on abuse.[26] Legal "employment bonds," a newly-minted version of quasi-indentured servitude and "liquidated damages" clauses in the employment contracts, all but ensure that the immigrant is at the mercy of the capitalists.[27] Less than half of H-1B employers sponsor immigrants for permanent residency status.[28] In 2014, Tata and Cognizant, the two largest H-1B visa recipients, sponsored 0 and 1 percent of their workers for green cards, respectively.[29] This effectively means that once the company is done with the migrant, they have no obligation to help them maintain status. Even in the "documented" context, capitalists can and have successfully divorced migrants from most means of legal and economic protection against exploitation.

The exploitation gig

While this tactic of profit protection through exploitation of a migrant's status has long been the norm, capitalists have found increasingly creative ways of adding citizens to the reserve army with minimal legal protections. Economics professor Anthony Gabb notes that the rise of the gig economy—nearly 40 percent of the US workforce—is evidence that the reserve army of labor has grown substantially.[30]

More than that, it is a means of capitalists like Uber and Amazon using the same tactics leveraged against migrants—low pay, abusive working conditions, and unstable employment—and applying them to the growing body of citizens in the now-global reserve army of labor.[31] What has long been true of migrants and their exploitation has come into force for citizen laborers, as Gabb notes—"[C]apitalism manufactures both wealth and unemployment (thereby inequality and misery), which is necessary for its own existence."[32]

It is ultimately not a question of whether technologies and automations are "good" or "bad" for reducing the necessary labor costs, any more than whether migrants and citizens can work alongside each other. Rather, it is a more fundamental question of who bears the risk and harm versus who retains the value of the labor. Under capitalism, the worker will always be in the former category and the capitalist in the latter. From 1979 to 2018, US workers' net productivity rose nearly 70 percent, while pay has only increased 11.6 percent.[33] As Professor Gabb notes—even as the reserve army of labor has grown, so has the wealth of the choice few, as has the chasm of inequality between the two.[34]

It is also at this crossroads, where the abuses of capitalism apply in some of the same fashion between both migrant and citizen, that the powers of xenophobia and racism can readily be weaponized. Immigrants, despite their role in padding capitalists' profits, become a source of competition, an enemy that is "stealing" American jobs, easy fuel for racist and xenophobic ideology. However, contrary to the rhetoric of migrants' job-stealing, it becomes evident that capitalists would gladly give them away, so long as it is profitable to do so. This is a demand of the system. If the reserve army of labor has a decreased ability to organize and fight back—either from depressed wages, intra-class strife, union busting, or the easy ability of capitalists to lay off and replace workers—so much the better.

As the contradictions within capitalism demand greater profitability with fewer costs, a need for expansion comes to bear—not just in territory, but in the availability of cheap human bodies.

Chapter 5

Empire and Immigration

In the summer of 2019, the media circulated a horrifying picture of Oscar Alberto Martinez Ramirez and his 2-year-old daughter Valeria lying face down on the bank of the Rio Grande, having drowned during a 1000-mile journey from El Salvador to seek asylum in the US. As always, the discussion on both left and right was largely devoid of the greater socio-political context in favor of a debate over cut-and-dry morality or legality. Deaths like those of Oscar and Valeria can easily be dismissed as a tragic attempt at skirting the law or that their flight from poverty and gang violence is not "America's problem."

A 2019 report from the Congressional Research Service presents a common understanding of the recent uptick in migrants fleeing the now infamous Northern Triangle (El Salvador, Guatemala, and Honduras) and what drives said migration—a mix of economic, environmental, political, and criminal factors.[1] The report claims that the Triangle's "long [history] of autocratic rule" and "corruption" combined with severely underfunded state institutions; natural disasters and food insecurity; and rampant transnational criminal organizations that terrorize the local populace all drive migration.[2] But Oscar and Valeria's deaths are part of the history of empire and capital in the Western Hemisphere. While migrants to the US come from all over the globe, this chapter explores the relationship between imperialism and migration in Central and South America, as it provides a clearer picture of one of the most contentious borderlines in the Americas.

Capitalism, empire, and Latin America

In his work on capitalist imperialism, Lenin predicted that as capital outgrew its internal market restraints, investors would look elsewhere to enrich themselves.[3] Imperialism is the highest stage of capitalism, a necessary expansion of the nation-state to gather new markets for itself and security against other nations doing the same.[4] Modern imperialism is the new face of colonizing the world. Not under the banner of God or the queen, but capital. The expansion of capital across the globe creates nation-state antagonisms which are only resolved by division and re-division of the world among a few imperial powers.[5]

The US's empire-building, both in economic and militaristic terms, has played a significant role in driving migrants to its borders on an increasingly global scale. The expansion of the US empire, despite the oft-used claims of being in the name of "democracy" and "freedom," has had little to do with either. It is a means of reproducing the economic system and the relationships therein.

Professor Greg Grandin details a long and tragic history of US involvement to the south in the forms of direct economic exploitation and military power.[6] As Grandin argues, this has fulfilled several roles, from opening up new markets to sharpening the imperialist axe for use elsewhere. In all instances, imperialism has had profound, likely unintended, consequences on migration as well as on the populace within the US border. These forces became synonymous with the very idea of America.

Latin America has been a prominent site of business expansion for over a century. In the early twentieth century Mexico alone had over a quarter of all American foreign investment.[7] This was part of the liberal zeal to make Manifest Destiny a reality, and when capital wasn't moving American superiority along fast enough, on more than one occasion, the nation-state moved to conquer land or outright buy it (e.g., Panama).[8] During the early 1900s, the US sent troops to Caribbean countries no less than 34 times.[9] From 1869 to 1897 it had sent warships into Latin American ports nearly 6000 times to protect US commercial interests and show off its prowess to Europe.[10]

By 1920, the US had started to fully flex its newfound imperial muscle. Latin America was fertile ground for absorbing raw materials, had key transit routes, and space for developing military strategy.[11] Imperialism replaced colonialism, as the latter could no longer accommodate the increasingly nationalistic tendencies of former colonies nor the nativist racism at home.[12] US imperialism in particular overcame these challenges by creating a united ideal of advancing prosperity at home by expanding America's economic and military power abroad.[13] The early part of the twentieth century solidified the groundwork for an enduring US imperial idea that inseparably tied together national security, international capitalism, and democratic "reform."[14] In this way, writes Grandin, an "empire's workshop" in Latin America "saved the United States from its own worst instincts" including dodging the capitalist-created Great Depression.[15]

This unified idea of capitalism and freedom (advanced at gunpoint) fully blossomed during the Cold War. The US used the ideology of spreading democracy and anti-Communist rhetoric to justify backing many of the destabilizing violent forces still at work today in Latin America—an ongoing cycle of US-backed coups, counter-insurgencies, and paramilitary death squads.[16] Emboldened corporations followed suit, even throwing support behind the death squads to quell any labor unrest.[17]

While the historical record is replete with many US interventions throughout the twentieth century, during Reagan's reign alone the administration committed over *a million dollars a day* to combat El Salvador's insurgents; launched the Contra affair in Nicaragua attempting to usurp the Sandinista revolution; and supported a genocidal Guatemalan military which, all told, left over 300,000 dead, thousands tortured, and millions fleeing.[18]

Capitalism would eventually make a "third conquest" of Latin America after it had been pacified through an often-violent imposition of free market fundamentalism.[19] Beginning in the 1980s, many of the Latin state-run systems, from schools to pensions, were auctioned off to capitalists from IBM to Citibank.[20] But neither this, nor any other push to open Latin countries' markets, served the purpose of creating democratic states or strong economies. Left with debt, violence, and wrecked economies, many nations were forced into de-socializing the last stable foundations of their society, creating a growing population of destitute people. A population of poor that went from 11 percent in the 1960s to over 30 percent in 2016.[21] Even under celebrated free trade agreements like the North American Free Trade Agreement (NAFTA), the working class suffered. NAFTA flooded Mexico with cheap imported goods, decimated manufacturing and small farming, drove millions from their land and pushed them northward towards available work.[22] Similar displacements happened in Central and South America.[23]

The US failure of instituting capitalist democracy by force is also apparent in Oscar and Valeria's home country of El Salvador, which demonstrates the ascension of widespread gang violence. The brutal Mara Salvatrucha gang, commonly known as the MS-13, originated in Los Angeles during the 70s and 80s; a gang that developed from an increasing population of young, stateless migrants fleeing El Salvador's US-fueled conflict.[24] The US then transplanted the gang to Central America in large numbers through the deportation process.[25] In 2010 alone, the US deported 120,000 gang members, most to the Northern Triangle.[26]

US imperialism kick-started and perpetuated an increasingly violent cycle of poverty, displacement, and a blurred line between criminal empires and corrupt state officials.[27] The existence of these capitalist-created nightmares, in turn, help keep the propaganda wheel turning by perpetuating the view of migrants and the violence they face in terms of US national security rather than a product of failed economic and military policy;

thus reducing US culpability and cementing the perception of migrants as threats.

Apart from the direct impacts of US empire, capitalism's sweep around the globe has also contributed to the growing climate crisis, which has, in turn, begun displacing people both in Central America and elsewhere. The World Bank estimates that there will be 143 million climate migrants by 2050.[28] In Latin America alone, it could be as high as 17 million.[29] Rising temperatures will destroy farmland, create water stress, and coupled with sea-level rise, will force already vulnerable people to move.[30]

Even if imperialism's displacement of people is an unintended consequence, it also has developed a benefit to capitalism—a vulnerable population of desperate people. A cheap and alienated workforce that comes to the empire, feeding and growing the global reserve army of labor. While there is not a grand unified conspiracy of capitalism and empire, their gears easily mesh together, creating a cycle of exploitation. As US imperialism disrupts economies, communities, and environments, driving people out of their homes, it also selectively benefits from the influx of cheap bodies. This influx demands greater resources for the state to exert control and so one continues to feed the other. Through both commercial and military means, a century of exploitation, intervention, and perpetuation of violence, US imperialism manufactured the instability that necessarily drove masses away from their birthplaces.

Empire's reign at home

Citizens are not free from the long reach of empire. US imperialism has also long acted as both a pressure valve and whetstone. Expansion has long served a smoothing function for internal working-class tensions. Grandin argues that imperialism helps shape and preserve the US national idea, a patriotism to latch onto that rises above working-class woes and diverts its view from its own plight to fight against "terror" or help "spread democracy."[31] This helps preserve political power in the hands of the few by distracting working people from the reality of how little control they have of their government.

More than that, the US empire's workshop in Latin America honed the sort of counter-insurgency ideas (freely and without regard for the human cost) later deployed against citizen workers, labor organizing, and protests within America's borders.[32] During the post-Vietnam period, domestic anti-militarism had grown significantly, and the US turned what it had learned in Latin America on its own citizens.[33]

Grandin describes an operation under Reagan that utilized intelligence techniques previously developed abroad to surveil political dissidents and intimidate them, as well as the creation of a counter-grassroots propaganda machine that would attempt to develop a pro-imperialist stance.[34] Activists were subject to harassment and even physical harm by Salvadoran death squads in Los Angeles.[35] The leaders of this government operation came to view rights like Miranda warnings and restrictions from surveillance by the nation-state as barriers to empire's progress.[36]

The current rhetoric used to flood the media with dubious ideas and patent falsehoods around immigration and a host of other issues has clear parallels to the Office of Public Diplomacy (since disbanded) created during this era. It obscured the US-backed human atrocities taking place in Central America to such a large degree that no anti-militarist/imperialist consensus could be formed.[37] Grandin details—"It was on the front line of the Central American conflicts that the Pentagon learned how to finesse the news at home by controlling reporters at the source."[38] This method of controlling the narrative that reaches the citizenry is now an established part of American foreign and domestic policy.[39] Ruling-class interests and ideology needed to be packaged in an appealing way—"Revolution in the name of democracy became a marketing device."[40]

It also rears its head well outside the imperial forum where it emerged—recently with climate change denial, where the supposed debate about science has taken a fundamentally political turn. Climate denialism is no longer about what the science says, but instead a form of propaganda to divert the revolutionary potential of climate change away from socialism.[41]

The use of force extends into the present as well. Police militarization and dispersal tactics against protesters have alarmingly similar parallels to imperialist tactics used abroad.[42] Police taunting protesters in Ferguson with "Whose streets? *OUR* streets!" rings with a similar emphasis on the civilian's lack of sovereignty as soldiers roam the streets of Baghdad.[43] The Pentagon's sale of military grade weapons and equipment to local police; SWAT's use of no-knock shock and awe tactics similar to those used to clear suspected insurgents' homes; the application of counter-insurgency doctrine to local "war(s) on crime"; the NYPD's military-style surveillance on Muslim residents in the post-9/11 era—are all fruits of a capitalist empire's development abroad.[44]

As Danny Sjursen, veteran of the Iraq war, notes, this is ultimately society's embrace of its "inner empire."[45] The ripples of imperialism touch on migrant and citizen alike. The consequences of imperialist tactics, both immediate and inevitable, like the waves of displaced people, will make their way back to the empire and its citizenry. The potential for slippage between the nation-state's subhuman treatment of migrants and its citizens is not only likely, but a common characteristic of a power wielded by the few, increasingly against the many.

Chapter 6

What is an Immigrant?

Having understood how capitalism and empire keep driving migrants to the US, a new problem comes into focus—that of control. While race, xenophobia, and even imperialism have played significant roles in shaping the *idea* of who is included in "American," they do not definitively answer the question of who is an immigrant. Deep down, past the questions of skin color and foreignness is necessarily the power to draw the lines. The *what* question here is how material reality gives rise to the power necessary to separate citizen from migrant and the ability to maintain that separation.

The social construct of an immigrant

Lorenzo Palma had lived in the US his whole life, his grandfather a native-born citizen of El Paso.[1] Shortly before his release on parole after serving 5 years for an assault conviction, immigration officials attempted to deport him. Despite believing he was a citizen, he could not *prove* that he was—his mother had traveled back to Mexico for his birth because she lacked the funds for an American hospital birth. After nearly 2 years of litigation (and detention), Palma obtained his grandfather's birth certificate and was able to demonstrate that he and his mother were US citizens at birth. Apart from questions of racial profiling, Palma's story illustrates that the entirety of someone's existence as an immigrant or citizen rests on a question of legality. And underlying the legal is a fundamental question of power.

The law is deeply unhelpful when attempting to define an immigrant. The Immigration Nationality Act defines an immigrant as any "alien" in the US and an "alien" as any person who is not a citizen or national of the US.[2] Thus, all immigrants are aliens and all aliens are noncitizens, unless they're not.

Unsurprisingly, the legal meaning of "immigrant" has no scientific basis as there are no biological means of determining who is an immigrant or not, despite a century of racialized approaches in the US. It is an abstraction that goes beyond describing someone's movement from place to place. It is a social construct that references a legal and political relationship between a person and a state apparatus. This relationship is independent of distance, and geography.

Consider Palma's scenario. Had he been born in El Paso, he would be a citizen, grandfather's citizenship aside. His grandfather's citizenship extended that status to him despite his birth on the other side of the border (a relatively short distance away). His mother could have traveled thousands of miles northward into Canada and produced the same outcome and possibly bestowed an additional citizenship on him.

Likewise, despite the white-nationalist dream, presently, there are no particular cultural or racial lines that legally distinguish between immigrant and citizen within America. Palma could have spoken only Spanish his entire life and practiced Buddhism; it would have made no difference as to his status as a citizen. While the aforementioned racial and cultural characteristics could be and have been used to inform immigration policy, the primary distinction and the one that carries overwhelming significance is the "legal" one, rather than particular physical or cultural characteristics. "Immigrant" in the modern context reflects the relationship of an individual to the nation-state. In order to fully grasp this relationship, it becomes necessary to understand the modern state's emergence and its relationship to capitalism.

The emergence of the nation-state

The modern nation-state, like the migrants it defines, arose out of the material realities of nascent capitalism. Under early capitalism, economic unification required political unity, something with superseding power over the old privileged feudal order. Marxist philosopher and economist Rosa Luxemburg argued that the national idea reflects the need of capitalists in each respective country for boundaries to establish their dominance of a market for its production.[3] The new ruling class needed to unify territories into a *fatherland* to establish both a labor market and consumer base. Economic interests gave birth to the political idea of the nation-state.[4]

This abstraction requires a strong military to protect itself; a force that also serves as a means to clear its way into the world market.[5] It also requires other bureaucratic and economic means of ruling over the mixed population of its territory.[6] Conflict is an inevitable result as different nationalities assert themselves over each other, moving from a defensive to an offensive position, from protecting their own unified identity to conquering and annexing their neighbors.[7]

The emergence of the nation-state during the Enlightenment superseded all historical concepts of ethnicity or even language in favor of voluntary political association.[8] The "patriots" of these movements were pursuing an overthrow of feudal lords in search of a nation to replace the old sovereigns.[9] This new order necessarily required new ideologies to liberate the working masses. As Marx noted, the values espoused in those revolutions became absolutes—"For each new class which puts itself in the place of one ruling before it, is compelled, merely in order to carry through its aim, to represent its interest as the common interest of all the members of society, that is, expressed in ideal form: it has to give its ideas the form of universality, and represent them as the only rational, universally valid ones."[10]

This is no less true of the American Revolution. While certainly possessing a variety of intermingled class forces and interests, the revolution's young elite class clearly fall into this framework of overthrow of feudal powers and taxation in favor of self-determination. For the revolutionary capitalists/pre-capitalists, the idea of equality was in the service of bucking the "divinely sanctioned social order," a liberation of the workforce for their enterprises by declaring all men "free."[11] The US Constitution was not a reflection of an absolute principle of equality for everyone, but a testament to this breaking with the old order and supplanting it with more universal, albeit elite, interests. Despite the seemingly universal nature of these abstract ideas, they too are historically bound, presented as a means of advancing one group's interests.

Political scientist Michael Parenti argues that, contrary to Enlightenment notions of true democracy and equality, the American Constitution's framers realized very quickly that the specter of a property-less majority was an existential threat to the established social order, and a national government was necessary to protect their class interests.[12] It was necessary to ensure that capitalists had a means of protecting themselves against outsiders, the working class, and each other by securing individual property rights and a means of addressing wrongs to those rights.[13]

Even the briefest of glances at US history reveals that the rights afforded by the Constitution were not conceptualized in a truly universal sense (e.g., slavery, women's suffrage, segregation). This is not to say that the principles of free speech, religious and ideological freedom, etc., are not worth pursuing. There were certainly progressive and democratic ideals that emerged from the Constitution. However, those principles were conceived in the protection of the status quo of social relations or were concessions won from class struggle. Even assuming the noble intentions of the drafters, their first concern was defending the interests of the wealthy few, of establishing their own power at the end of the revolution, and all concessions made to the people were driven, as Parenti notes — "not by a love of democracy, but by a fear of it."[14]

The nation-state is far more than the enshrinement of ruling-class ideas of governance. As Louis Althusser argued—because it arises within and for capitalism, it is an idea given form in the repressive means of state control over the working class.[15] This is accomplished either by force or by ideology but stems from the state's ability to exercise unilateral power over the people under its control all in the service of reproducing itself and the economic basis for its existence.[16] Immigration judges, ICE, the border walls, and even the Constitution are manifestations of the nation-state's power to control and divide people for the sake of preserving the current class relationships under capitalism.

The nation-state, the immigrant, and us

As the ruling class needed to unify differing ethnic and cultural groups under a national idea, so too emerged the need to predicate the us/them distinction on something other than those same groups. As Malik notes, the concept of the foreigner was ill-defined prior to the emergence of nationalism.[17] The history of the very word "immigrant" appeared alongside capitalism's rapid development during the eighteenth century, and its meaning took on the characteristics of "space, time, purpose."[18]

From the outset, the national idea was unable to develop a truly unified people as it carried an inherent contradiction. Enlightenment conceptions of human beings endowed with universal rights were necessarily constrained by the fact that they were citizens of different nations.[19] The idea of a truly free individual was boxed-in by the requirements of her "citizenship" as part of the nation that helped establish freedoms for its people.[20] Malik argues that this tension and inability to overcome national divisions caused both nations and divisions to be seen as natural.[21]

This inability to bring about a truly universal conception of rights independent of nationality is now so pervasive that there is no ready way to discuss or even conceive of a person or peoples in any socio-political context without using words like "immigrant," "American," or "European." These are not just geographical locators but are verbal representations of a body of rights. The rights enshrined in America's founding documents, which so many see as universal, are actually tied to and dictated by an individual's relationship to the nation-state.

Returning to Palma's story—his mother, grandfather, his citizen and noncitizen neighbors are not governed by absolute, democratic, and universalist principles of life, liberty, or due process. Rather, these are informed by a particular class conception of those principles as applied to the collective; a conception that ultimately ensures that the majority of political and economic power remains in the hands of a few. The current immigration machine did not emerge and does not exist to sort humanitarian necessity, exceptional people, or those worthy of and willing to pursue the American Dream. It is in service of ruling-class interests and is a means of shoring up sovereign power over both migrants and citizens. Neither the migrant nor the citizen define the US as a nation. *It* defines *them*.

This distinction is made even more stark by returning to the fundamental inquiry in Palma's case—what *makes* him a US citizen? It is not a commitment to a certain ideology, a cultural identity, or religious belief, despite how these aspects play into each person's conception of self as Americans. The all-important question is whether Palma or anyone else can assume the rights (limited as they may be) of an American; a question of whether the nation-state has bestowed them. In the present birthright scheme of citizenship, it is someone who is either born within the construct of America, whether that is its borders (and sometimes colonies); to American parents; or permissively (though not fully) assimilated into the citizenry by meeting certain naturalization requirements.

The ability to decide who is or is not included in the political body, endowed with the rights of a citizen, is at the heart of the state's sovereign power and the present economic system it protects. As Palma's case plainly illustrates, citizenship, *personhood* is rooted in something as unmerited and unalterable as his birth. Should he have made the ill-advised choice to pick a different set of parents and grandparents, the outcome of his 2-year battle could have turned out quite differently.

What follows in the coming chapters is how sovereign power and capitalism are interlaced with the US immigration system; how dehumanization is essential to perpetuating that power, and how citizens, like migrants, have little say in how it is wielded.

Chapter 7

The Southern Border and Sovereign Power

In 2018, a jury acquitted US Border Patrol Agent Lonnie Swartz of second-degree murder and involuntary manslaughter after he shot and killed 16-year-old Jose Antonio Elena Rodriguez through the border fence in Nogales, Arizona.[1] Swartz, standing on the US side, fired at Jose 16 times through the fence, 13 of which were while Jose was face down on the ground.[2] Swartz claimed he feared for his and other officers' lives—he alleged that a 16-year-old boy was throwing rocks (which Border Patrol considers lethal weapons) 60 feet up over the border fence.[3] Despite this claim, there was little evidence that if rocks were thrown, Jose was the one doing the thowing.[4] While Swartz is facing a civil suit, he, among other similarly-situated Border Patrol Agents, has argued that Jose did not have Constitutional protections, as the boy was not a US citizen nor on US soil.[5] As discussed below, the Supreme Court seems inclined to agree.

This is but one of the myriad of evils that crops up at the border, a place that has re-emerged as a fixation in the American mind. It is here, at the US border, where the lines of humanity and nonpersonhood are blurred and where sovereign power is most firmly rooted.

The lines that shape us

There is nothing natural about borders.[6] In the modern context, they are both formed by their relationship to capitalism and work to protect it. The US border's key function is establishing the self-granting power of a sovereign (the nation-state) to control those within its territory[7] and by extension, to establish who is a citizen. The border is a necessary extension of the nation-state, and as it relates to migrants, a means of focusing and controlling migrant bodies. It is both a fixed position and a fluid one, both physical and ideological, representative of the limits of human rights and the ability to deny them. The border is "not a natural nor neutral practice, but one that serves to benefit those whose interests are bound up in maintaining the status quo."[8]

As Grandin writes in *The End of the Myth*, the US border has always existed as a contradiction—a simultaneous closing off from the world, of protecting the nation-state and those it allows to labor under it, while also demonstrating limitless power, influence, and expansion.[9] The border, both as an open and closed concept, has been used throughout US history as a means of control.

The concept of a boundless border emerged in the earliest moments of America. Madison, among other Constitutional drafters, recognized the need to pacify working-class power and saw the expansion into the frontier as a means of diffusing class tensions.[10] This included expanding "democracy" and "freedom" for the newly liberated white Americans, which soared to new heights through the extermination of first peoples and the theft of their lands; it was through the pacification of the frontier that the white working class won and maintained its freedoms.[11] This reality should be familiar by now, one that has echoes in slavery and indentured servitude—the earliest American understood his rights and freedoms by setting himself apart from others, often by subjugating or exploiting them.

Expansion not only served its purpose of ensuring working-class pliability but also fueled incredible capitalist growth—from 1900 to the Cold War, the US outpaced most of the developing world's consumption despite having a small relative population.[12] The border built the concept of American superiority, one that could be recycled nearly indefinitely and acted as a safety valve[13] against class tensions.

In the post WWII era, this narrative of expansion took a new character, one of seeking an "open" world.[14] At the same moment of espousing this rhetoric, the US erected the first barrier along the border with Mexico using chain link fencing re-purposed from Japanese internment.[15] In doing so, it ushered in a new era of horrors against migrants at the fringes of political life. The contradiction between America's push for global openness and growing internal tensions under capitalism pushed the violence to the literal borders of society and politics, where it had room to vent on a people reduced to the subhuman.[16]

The border still possesses a promise of prosperity and expansion, albeit to a lesser and darker degree. There is a growing industrial complex that has shot-up around the border wall— contractors SLSCO and Barnard Construction have won over $400 million in wall-construction contracts in 2018 alone.[17] The labor-migration industry, referred to as "migration merchants," is an incredibly profitable business and one that has *grown* with increased border controls.[18] This is in addition to the migrant detention-industrial complex that has been wildly lucrative for a number of companies (explored more fully in a coming chapter on migrant criminalization).

But more than the saplings of profit reminiscent of a bygone era, the fetishism with the border and its enforcement has grown exponentially as has its function as a violent outlet and repository of racism and brutality. Greater than the promise of prosperity, the border reveals the very basis of sovereign power.

Border brutality and *bare life*

Swartz is merely one officer in a long line of brutal people guarding the frontier. The founding individuals of Customs and Border Patrol (then under the Department of Labor), having lost the national debate about keeping Mexican labor out of the country altogether, was comprised largely of white supremacists.[19] The present evils of family separation, coerced confessions (including "stress" techniques later associated with the US military in Iraq), and extrajudicial killings of migrants by Border Patrol all return to its 1924 racist origins, which included murder and torture of migrants from the outset.[20] At the time, Border Patrol's abuse even had a direct element of labor exploitation—they would deliver immigrants to farms in exchange for hunting and fishing favors and then would come back and raid those same farms, thereby giving the farmers free labor since they need not pay the incarcerated and imminently deportable migrants.[21]

Grandin notes that this cycle of terrible violence has a material essence. The impossible task of policing the border is necessarily representative of the insurmountable gap between the massive accumulation of wealth and desperate poverty.[22] As global capitalism destabilizes communities all over the world, border enforcement will continue to demand an increasingly militant and violent force (both state and vigilante) to hold-off the human consequences.

Of course, this violence does little to drive back the masses. As the Italian delegates at the Socialist Congress of 1907 long ago noted—"One cannot fight migrants, only the abuses which arise from emigration…*we know that the whip of hunger that cracks behind migrants is stronger than any law made by governments.*"[23] (emphasis mine). This is evident in border crossings. Apprehensions have dropped over the last decade and a half, largely due to economic factors rather than the intense cruelty of border enforcement.

The militarization of the border has only succeeded in increasing migrant deaths. Since 2003 Border Patrol has killed 97 people with almost no prosecutions, Swartz being an exception.[24] From 1999 through 2012, Border Patrol has exploded from 4208 to 21,394 officers and the immigrant death toll has climbed right along with it—increasing by more than 80 percent, despite overall illegal entries declining by 77 percent.[25] In 2012, when unlawful crossings were on the decline, a migrant was *eight times more likely to die in the attempt* than 10 years before.[26]

The overall decrease in migrant apprehensions also belies the shift in the kinds of migrants at America's border as a result of the consequences of imperialism. In the past, many undocumented entrants to the US were single men economically displaced by things like NAFTA; but as the US economy faltered in the mid-aughts, labor-based migration slowed.[27]

Contrast this with the statistics of family migration—in February 2019, over 66,000 (65 percent) of border apprehensions consisted of family units or unaccompanied minors, compared to the 3 percent of family units from February 2013.[28] As the Department of Homeland Security (DHS) admits, many of the families are not trying to disappear into the shadows but are turning themselves in, seeking refuge.[29] The southern border and its enforcers are not holding back waves of terrorists, criminals, or even "job-stealing" migrants, but broken and desperate families fleeing failed US policy in Latin America.

When paired together, the violence leveled at the growing number of refugees is a reflection of sovereign power's origins. Swartz's and the multitude of other Border Patrol extrajudicial killings and historically oppressive acts help paint the contours of where life actually has any significance, as being worthy of protection. A 2020 Supreme Court case involving another CBP cross-border killing ruled that the family of the slain boy did not have standing to sue the agent or the agency—Constitutional protections simply do not apply in these instances.[30] Had this case been decided prior to Swartz's prosecution, he likely would have avoided a trial altogether. This is the very nature of sovereign power, a reduction of people to what philosopher Giorgio Agamben terms *bare life*—beings who we recognize as living, but who are devoid of any rights, any access to a true democratic voice, stripped of a life worth living.[31]

It is at the border where the last vestiges of any hope of political and democratic protection fade and the lines are blurred between protected and unprotected life. Recent court precedent notwithstanding, the 100-mile area around the border has long been considered what the American Civil Liberties Union terms a "constitution-free zone."[32] As Grandin writes—

> There have been contradictory judicial rulings, but historically, agent power has been limited by no constitutional clause. There are few places patrollers can't search, no property belonging to migrants they can't seize. And there is hardly anybody they can't kill, provided that the victims are poor Mexican or Central American migrants.[33]

Border Patrol "rejects any geographic limitation on agents' authority"[34] and consistent with the Supreme Court's recent decision, has good reason to. What this gap between enforcement and results together with the attendant violence reveals about the border is not just its uselessness as a protective barrier, but the link between bare life and sovereign power.

Bare life is the means by which the nation-state establishes its own sovereign power—by removing itself from the laws it uses to mercilessly reduce people to this form of existence.[35] As scholar Thomas Carl Wall notes—"The essence of political power in the West...is the power to suspend (not apply) law and thus to produce a sphere of beings without quantities, homines sacri, whom ever being, insofar as he or she is alive, may be."[36] The border provides the means to suspend the protections extended to the citizen, and through the brutality that follows in its wake provides something more—the means to legitimize itself.[37]

In Swartz's case, even if any and all of the proceedings are resolved in the victim's favor, it is precisely at the point that this power can choose whether or not to exempt him and any other that the paradox of sovereignty is manifest—it is both inside and outside the system of laws; by exempting itself from accountability, it creates the space for the law to be valid.[38] Sovereign power is not only the power to decide what life can be taken without consequences but ultimately, where life has any political relevance.[39]

While the abstract nature of sovereign power and the bare life it creates are difficult to grasp, both will become clearer as the dehumanizing facets of modern immigration are laid out. Suffice it for now, this power (and the status quo it protects) requires bare life to perpetuate itself,[40] and the US has found a seemingly unending supply of it, just beyond the border.

The far reach of America's border

Despite being held out as fixed in nature, borders are anything but, both historically and currently. As capitalism has increased its reach around the globe, borders too have evolved to a point where, as scholar Nick Vaughan-Williams points out, a nation's borders are no longer at the border.[41] The growing global "security" network found intercepting people at airports and in homes looks to move beyond the immediate realm of its territory to target the "outsider" long before she reaches US shores.[42] In 2019, Mexico, caving to pressure from the US, agreed to deploy its national guard to turn back migrants headed northward at its own southern border; essentially an extension of the US's own enforcement.[43] Borders have become "portable machines of sovereign power."[44]

As a line between peoples, the sovereign power that emanates from the border can inevitably be leveraged over the citizens supposedly under its protection. The 100-mile border zone effects far more than the migrants at its edges—roughly two-thirds (nearly 200 million people) of the US population lives within this zone along US land or coastal borders.[45] Border Patrol operates about 170 interior checkpoints throughout the country,[46] which, Constitution or not, provide Border Patrol with the opportunity to conduct all manner of search and interrogation, regardless of grounded suspicion. Increasingly, the profit motive has driven the development of tracking and identification systems, amongst other technologies, spurring on the growing militarization of the border zone.[47] Even Border Patrol played its part in growing the US national security apparatus by teaching allied security forces in counter-insurgency tactics.[48]

The border's ideological strength stands in a morass of contradictions; those in power have long leveraged it against others that might challenge the sovereign power the border evokes. During and post WWI, labor unions faced serious state crackdowns, anti-war protesters were beaten, and all other manner of perceived anti-Americanism was attacked;[49] all while border expansion was held out as a means of moving past "sectional loyalties."[50]

The border also functioned as a means of keeping out foreign influence such as the Universal Declaration of Human Rights for fear that the growing internationalism after WWII would lead to social rights that would threaten the free market system.[51] Reagan leveraged the growing radical nationalism (particularly amongst Vietnam veterans) around the border to sell the idea of the Cold War actions in Latin America, which in turn, drove more migrants to the border, starting the cycle of enflaming white-nationalist passions all over again.[52]

The horrors of migrant deaths in the desert, their murder at the hands of Border Patrol and vigilante groups are all deeply tied to sovereign power and its reach, linked to the suffering that imperialism imposes on its citizens. There is a direct citizen corollary to Border Patrol killings and the general lack of accountability—the all-too routine police killings of people of color within the US. The sovereign power that absolved Swartz and his contemporaries of responsibility is the same that releases the vast majority of police from their roles in the deaths of black citizens. When black lives can be taken without consequence, just like migrants in the desert, both are reduced to bare life.

There is also a dark irony at play in the border's influence over its citizens, elucidated by a veteran with a brain injury and stress disorder in one of the border vigilante groups—the group provides him with a place to belong, a means of calming his nightmares and creating new memories.[53] It is precisely at the cause of collective suffering that people seek relief from the alienation they experience under capitalism and its shadows, albeit by perpetuating its violence. As one CBP agent noted in the wake of the refugees fleeing NAFTA's aftershocks — America "increasingly defines itself by what it hates."[54]

The border as the site of bare life and sovereign power creates a cycle — bare life provides an easy scapegoat, a nonperson, where an alienated citizenry can direct its fury and blame for their own suffering under capitalism, leaving the unquestioned exercise of power in the hands of a few. The border is a means of producing and controlling the layer of bodies capitalism uses to keep its head above water. The US border does not keep its citizens safe from migrants. It keeps capitalism safe from the people it dominates.

Chapter 8

ICE and National Security

In 2018, ICE targeted and detained Ravi Ragbir, an undocumented leader of the immigrant rights group New Sanctuary Coalition of New York City, intending to enforce a prior deportation order.[1] He and his family had (like many others) faced a decade of probation-esque "check-ins" with ICE, under the constant threat of removal.[2] Ravi has been fighting a wire fraud conviction since 2001, but had been ordered removed by an immigration judge.[3] During the check-in, Ravi fainted after being told ICE was trying to remove him, and had to be transported by ambulance.[4] A total of 18 protesters, including two city council members, were arrested as they formed a wall around the ambulance and impeded its path.[5]

This story is a tragically common outcome of migrant interactions with ICE—the looming threat of detention, separation of families, and the possibility of not even getting a chance to say goodbye. ICE itself is a relatively new construct (a mere 15 years old) born of the "opportunistic and frenzied political reorganization that happened in the wake of the attacks of September 11, 2001."[6] As part of the massive Department of Homeland Security, which is the conglomeration of 22 federal agencies and 170,000 federal employees,[7] ICE stands out as a particular villain, with its abuses being some of the most visible in communities throughout the US. ICE is the cross section of questions of capitalism, terrorism and national security, and how abusive and arbitrary power is justified to the powerless.

Moral panic and migration

Congress passed the PATRIOT Act in the wake of the "moral panic" that followed 9/11. A moral panic is a perceived societal threat that can radically change social values, often by demanding a return to prior ones (in effect, reactionary by nature).[8] Those in power can leverage these panics to pursue their own ends.[9] In a post-9/11 America, the Bush administration and its capitalist cohort (with help from the media) were able to pass the PATRIOT Act, launch an endless, pointless, and profitable war on terror, and at the center of it all, brand a lasting enemy in America's very midst—immigrants.[10]

Immigrants, by their very nature of being outsiders, could not be trusted and thus fit in perfectly with the narratives built around a moral panic. The nature of ICE and DHS is representative of the PATRIOT Act's very core—a codified notion that the "other" is a constant, fundamental threat to America's existence and lives both within and without America's borders. In order to justify a massive intrusion on civil liberties; expenditures for immigration enforcement that, by 2013, had superseded *all other federal criminal law enforcement agencies combined;*[11] and the creation of a massive detention network—the ruling class needed and found a ready scapegoat. By branding migrants as enemies, shifting the governance of them from articles of commerce incident to sovereignty to a focus of *national security,* the US politicized them in an unprecedented way—in opposition to its very existence.

This politicization is an assurance that the divisions between citizen and bare life are increasingly difficult to erase—Ravi, despite his long history in the community, his family, and the possibility of innocence, could be disregarded at whim. The PATRIOT Act and its enforcers have weaponized migrants in a way that ensures not only that those lines are tolerated, but more importantly, create an increased demand to protect "us" from "them."

ICE works to destabilize migrant families and communities, all but guaranteeing that their bodies, labor, and voices remain under the thumb. ICE and DHS are a means of bringing the war on terror and terror itself to America's neighborhoods; of separating out bare life from all others, one city street at a time. For the migrant, this terror has little-to-no political or legal remedy. As is evident in Ragbir's case, ICE has newfound courage to carry-out direct political attacks to remove challenges to its power. Increasingly, it uses detention and deportation to suppress open political dissent. Other immigrant activists, including the 22-year-old Daniela Vargas, Jose Enrique Balcazar Sanchez, Zully Victoria Palacios Rodriguez, and a growing number of others across the US have been arrested by either ICE or CBP in an apparent attempt to silence any outspoken undocumented voices.[12] The war on migrants and the accumulation of power necessary to carry it out has become increasingly blatant in its moves towards cementing itself, with money trailing close behind.

The profit of national security

This accumulation of power invites profit potential and helps feed a number of private industries including the prison-industrial complex and, increasingly, the data and surveillance industries. ICE deploys several technologies in its war on migrants. One such technology is Stingray, which simulates cell phone towers that trick nearby phones into transmitting information about location and identification. The Harris Corporation, the maker of the Stingray, has successfully marketed the device to ICE as well as law enforcement nationwide.[13] In 2016 DHS had over 124 of these devices and had spent over $24 million apart from the $1.8 million it had doled out in grants to state and local law enforcement for purchasing the devices.[14] Each device can cost from $41,500 to as high as $500,000.[15]

More mainstream companies like Amazon increasingly aid in ICE's reduction of migrants to the subhuman. Despite Jeff Bezos's criticism of Trump's policies, Amazon's web services (AWS) house Palantir, a data-mining company used by everyone from the military, to the CIA, FBI, and DHS.[16] Palantir has over $150 million in contracts with ICE alone.[17] Palantir assists ICE in gathering and amassing vast amounts of information from utility bills, healthcare information, biometric databases, and even cell phone records.[18] This same technology is growing in use by local law enforcement, who are essentially assisting ICE in building its massive database.[19]

Unsurprisingly, the use of these technologies against migrants will inevitably overshadow the US citizenry as well. Stingray inevitably picks up information from other nearby cell phones and is gaining a foothold in local law enforcement units around the US.[20] The Tucson Police Department alone purchased at least $400,000 worth of Stingray equipment in 2014.[21] The vast amounts of data that Palantir collects and compiles already intersects with local law enforcement and grows daily with information well outside the confines of immigration enforcement. These functions will increasingly blur the lines between the "foreign" and "local" threats as they relate to power—the weapons deployed against migrants will find their way back to citizens.

Terror, Security, and Justifications of Power

This erosion of civil liberties and the profiteering thereof are often justified in terms of the security state's "war on terror" and making America safer. Even assuming the most noble of intentions, what both ICE and the national-security apparatus incorrectly assume and argue, is that enforcement is a path towards destroying terrorism in the US and globally. For example, ICE's then-Assistant Secretary Michael Garcia noted in a 2005 address—"Are criminal prosecutions enough? Clearly not...We still must approach terrorist cells and plots...with traditional enforcement tools, albeit in new ways."[22] There is a pervasive and persistent myth that the nation can fight its way to suppressing the violence poverty creates.

The means of targeting internal terrorism (read: primarily

migrant terrorists) has been not only ineffectual but, strangely, self-generated—of the hundreds of people charged with terrorism-related cases since 2001, researchers discovered that *all but four* of the high-profile domestic terrorism plots leading up to 2014 "were actually FBI sting operations—plots conducted with the direct involvement of law enforcement informants or agents, *including plots that were proposed or led by informants.*"[23] (emphasis mine). Even within the traditional law enforcement context this approach is disturbing, as one former agent noted—"When the FBI undercover agent or informant is the only purported link to a real terrorist group, supplies the motive, designs the plot and provides all the weapons, one has to question whether they are combating terrorism *or creating it.*"[24] (emphasis mine).

What this failed approach reveals, as journalist and activist Masha Gessen notes in her book on the Boston bombers, is that when it comes to terrorists, people and governments understand very little—terrorists are not depressed, or radicalized fanatics, or emotionally disturbed, but rather are disturbingly *normal.*[25] What is known, according to terrorism expert Louise Richardson, is that what appears to push people to violence is not just a sense of poverty or deprivation but is ultimately a question of their position relative to others;[26] arguably a question of class position.

The security state's belief in the flawed idea of radicalization ignores the material basis of terrorism. The forces of global capital and its accompanying imperialism have spread not just exploitation and poverty throughout the planet, but also a growing understanding of the massive gap between classes and with it, the inevitable tensions that accompany them.[27] Poverty and inequality provide the fertile grounds for terrorism to take root.[28] The security state not only fails to meaningfully address (or even acknowledge) these core issues, but ultimately, characteristic of its capitalist origins, perpetuates them.

It should be unsurprising that the US's war on migrants and terror (in effect, two sides of the same coin) has not made and will not make anyone safer. Even assuming there are immigrant terrorists in America's midst, from a purely strategic standpoint, it makes little sense to deport them back to their countries where they still have the means of organizing attacks from abroad.[29] Practically speaking, as of June 2018, the vast majority of ICE arrests (79 percent) were migrants with no criminal record (58 percent) or a minor offense (such as a traffic violation), (21 percent).[30]

This comes either at the expense or willful ignorance of other acts of terror, as the security state either ignores or minimizes the growing threat and acts of local terror from white nationalists. This is not to say that a security state is even necessary to fight repugnant ideologies but rather to indicate that if its true mission is to reduce all forms of terrorism, it is not only failing, but ignoring a growing source of it among its citizens.[31] Instead, the national security apparatus, true to its roots in sovereign power, needs something to justify its existence — in this case, cultivating an ongoing moral panic against immigrants.

The failures and inconsistencies of ICE and DHS's approach point to a circular system — it continues feeding a monster of its own creation in order to justify its fight against that monster. The use of terror and moral panics are one of the strategies for social control within the internal bounds of the nation-state, a means of valorizing the security state. The politicization of migrants is a consolidation of power and preservation of the status quo. It is using the "threat" of migrants to exert control over everyone within America's borders. One of the most prescient dangers within the security state is the elimination of limited transparency and the already thin democratic means of demanding accountability of the state to its people. Foreign Intelligence Surveillance Act courts, the National Security Agency, and the growing technologies like Palantir reveal that the justifications of the security state not only rest on shaky ground, but more fundamentally, operate increasingly outside of both migrants' and citizens' ability to challenge it.

The result is that the exercise of this power has become increasingly brazen. Returning to Ravi's case, it was only an act of sheer legal prowess that prevented ICE from disappearing him out of the country (he was already on a plane to Florida when his lawyers secured a habeas order).[32] The growing gap between power and the democratic means of challenging it is terrifyingly evident in the judge's opinion ordering Ravi's release from ICE custody. The judge acknowledged that while the state's right to deport him is uncontested, it did not have a right to do so cruelly—"[Ravi] is entitled to the freedom to say goodbye."[33]

While undoubtedly a noble gesture, it demonstrates the very limits of human decency as it relates to migrants—that the sum total of the due process afforded to them in the face of ICE's brutality is the ability to hug their children one last time before being torn away, possibly forever. This gap reflects the very fragility of everyone's rights under such rule, the brokenness of American democracy that cedes all but the last goodbye to the manifestations of power, the resignation that there is nothing more to be done in the face of such terrible acts except to ensure they aren't exceptionally cruel.

If terrorism, at its core, is "the deliberate creation and exploitation of fear through violence or the threat of violence in pursuit of political change,"[34] ICE commits an act of terror daily.

Chapter 9

Migrant Criminalization

Eduardo Jose Garza had been in the US for 14 years, with a wife and three children.[1] The police detained him during a traffic stop and turned him over to ICE. Rather than him appear in immigration court, however, authorities brought him to federal court in McAllen, Texas, charged with the crime of improper entry together with 48 other immigrants. He faced up to 6 months of federal prison time. After Eduardo's court-appointed attorney told him to plead guilty "so they would deport [him] as quickly as possible," the judge sentenced him to 4 months and then ICE removed him from the US. His pregnant wife continued to make ends meet through the help of neighbors, patient landlords, and by selling homecooked food. Garza returned as quickly as he could but missed the birth of his child.

This is the daily face of Operation Streamline, the poisonous fruition of the early twentieth century laws criminalizing migrants.[2] This chapter explores how these statutes are used to funnel migrants into the prison-industrial complex, how the protections of due process fail to protect migrants against human warehousing, and ultimately, how the reach of the sovereign power necessary to do all of it extends well beyond this "internal enemy."

Streamlining prison profits

Under 8 USC sections 1325 and 1326, an immigrant's improper entry (anywhere other than the places set out by immigration authorities) is a misdemeanor; re-entry after being deported or denied entry is a felony. These are the primary statutes the government uses to convict migrants in Streamline cases. Through Streamline, migrants are fast-tracked through the criminal process, which charges and sentences as many as 70 people a day.[3]

For the misdemeanor cases, prosecutors use a combination of plea offers and harsh sentencing alternatives to essentially force migrants to plead guilty and relinquish their appellate rights.[4] Felony re-entry cases can carry sentence enhancements up to 20 years, which places them at a higher federal classification than an assault with the threatened use of a gun.[5] In these felony cases, prosecutors offer most immigrant defendants the ability to plead down to the misdemeanor improper entry charge, reducing jail time to 6 months or less.[6] This bargain, 6 months versus a possible 20 years, all but guarantees a plea, with the immigrant giving up the right to trial or appeal.[7]

Unlike civil immigration removal proceedings, criminalized migrants have access to counsel. This protection, however, is mostly worthless in practice as the process hamstrings defense attorneys. Few, if any, migrants are willing to challenge the charges (the prosecutors' burden of proof in re-entry cases amounts to demonstrating the defendants are physically present in the US and submitting a record of their prior deportation[8]) and most forgo their rights for more lenient sentencing. The legal challenges to this process have been constrained to ensuring that judges ask each person individually if the migrant understood his or her rights, rather than in a group.[9]

As Eduardo himself puts it—"I have children here and everything and it's impossible to stay there [in Mexico] and leave my children here."[10] Whatever the stated intent about the deterrent effect of prosecutions (it has little[11]) or the subjective ideology of politicians that a crackdown will free up political space to enact reform (it clearly hasn't), Streamline is firmly bound up in the capitalist/migrant cycle of exploitation. As one Streamline judge notes: "[The] current flood of prosecutions are only happening because we've created all these opportunities for immigrants so we can enjoy the benefit of their cheap labor."[12]

In 2004, the US government prosecuted nearly 40,000 in this fashion.[13] By the end of the Bush era, that number had jumped to nearly 80,000, and under Obama, at its height, nearly 100,000.[14] Migrant criminal prosecutions made up *over 50 percent* of all federal prosecutions in 2016.[15] That same year, nearly a quarter of the Federal Prison population were noncitizens and nearly 750,000 have been criminally prosecuted for improper migration since 2005.[16] Of course, the costs are extraordinary — it costs $30,000 per year to incarcerate someone,[17] an amount that, ironically, the US could pay to an individual to stay in their birthplace and sit on her hands for an entire year and she would be exponentially above the global poverty line.[18]

This money is funneled to a lucrative private-prison industry that includes the Corrections Corporation of America and the GEO Group. Between them, there is over $3.2 *billion* in annual revenue, which continues to grow.[19] This grotesque capitalist industry naturally demands expansion and has contracts in place for occupancy guarantees[20] which require minimum amounts of inmates or the state must pay fees for unused beds. Similarly, the industry spends millions in lobbying to ensure that demand is not decreased by the "relaxation of enforcement efforts, leniency in conviction or parole standards and sentencing practices..."[21]

This demand for more bodies has been accomplished through Streamline, ICE detainment, and the infamous 287(g) program. 287(g) is an agreement between ICE and local state law enforcement that deputizes the latter as federal immigration agents. Local law enforcement then arrests and turns any alleged noncitizens over to ICE.[22] Apart from the direct benefit to the private-prison industry, 287(g) counties (often in southern states) now have a legal means of combating what they see as a threat, despite the fact that a majority of the immigrants they detain are guilty of traffic or other low-level offenses.[23]

Thus, there is a terrible duality played out at the expense of the migrant. Profit and its increasing demands perpetuate this grotesque form of exploitation where actual human beings are poured in and out of private jails as commodities. But it relies on the criminal processes that necessarily seek to exclude and remove migrants from social and political life altogether.

Due process and sovereign power

The civil immigration detention process is even more fraught than the criminal one. Despite the terminology, the civil process lacks even the most basic protections against arbitrary confinement. In its 2018 decision *Jennings v. Rodriguez*, the Supreme Court determined that in many instances (including asylum seekers), the INA *requires* detention of migrants throughout the duration of their removal proceedings, without any particular right to a bond hearing within a specified period.[24]

While the court ultimately left open the question of the overall constitutionality of the INA when it returned the case to the lower court, Justice Breyer noted in his dissent that the majority's interpretation would seem to undermine the protections of the 5th Amendment.[25] As one law journal notes, by bending to the other powers of the state, the court effectively "stifled the clearest route to due process protections for noncitizens who have been detained for excessively long periods of time...[T]he end result will likely be minimal protections against indefinite detention for noncitizens."[26]

The *Jennings* decision stems from a long-standing legal fiction that the immigration process—particularly detention and deportation—is civil and therefore free of any punitive characteristics.[27] The Supreme Court has justified immigrant detention in terms of its relationship to removal proceedings—it cannot be a punishment since it is only being deployed to ensure the accused shows up to her hearing, rather than punishing her for a crime.[28] As one scholar notes—"Rather than engaging in a nuanced balancing of life, liberty, or property interests, immigration law's traditional approach simply treats certain aliens as nonpersons to whom the Due Process Clause does not apply."[29] Thus, the detained migrant is caught in a shadow between legal worlds, treated in practice as a wrongdoer but not criminalized such that limited Constitutional protections would apply.

And it is this aspect of migrant detention that is actually an expression of sovereign power and bare life—what Agamben refers to as the "zone of indistinction"—the space where the law is suspended and the lines are blurred between qualified (politically protected) and bare life.[30] As scholar Judith Butler explored in her discussion of Agamben against the backdrop of indefinite detention in Guantánamo, this power relies upon nothing other than the "deeming" of certain forms of life to be ineligible for certain basic human rights: "the decision to detain, to continue to detain someone indefinitely, is a unilateral judgement made by government officials who simply deem that a given individual, or indeed a group, poses a danger to the state."[31] The ability to decide that one cage is punishment and the other is merely procedural is sovereign power (and its attendant bare life) exercised at its fullest.

Taken together, the criminalization and detention of migrants serves a number of capitalist and ruling-class interests. It provides not only a means of recurring profit but also ensures migrant pliability, as a criminal conviction, together with the civil "bars" for repeat improper entries, will likely forever haunt his or her ability to move towards a "legal" status. The exercise of sovereign power in the zone of indistinction, the creation of bare life, is a means of domination over everyone under its reach.

The jailing of migrants, essentially a crime of where they were born, is not just a question of control over them, but ultimately weakens the citizen's own position as it relates to power—"That a group of individuals held within our borders may be detained indefinitely, without an individualized finding of necessity, cannot be reconciled with the concept of due process. To attempt to do so would diminish the meaning of due process for us all."[32] Sovereign power, especially as wielded for the benefit of the few, can shape the very contours of what is "due" from due process.

The long arm of profit and power

Despite the boon that criminalized migrants create for the prison-industrial complex, it is inevitable that the institution extends its reach beyond migrant bodies and communities. Depressed rural American communities, particularly those impacted by NAFTA, see the prisons as a means of alleviating poverty, unemployment, and general decline.[33] Despite their perception as beneficial in these poor areas, prisons serve the interests of capital. As abolitionist and prison scholar Ruth Gilmore puts it—they are "geographical solutions to political economic crisis," a way for capitalism to reabsorb the idle people, land, and capital.[34]

Despite the short-term economic lift these human warehouses provide, they carry dangers that perpetuate the cycle of poverty. In order to entice (and essentially sponsor) a prison's development, communities must inevitably pull resources away from social welfare and public services towards incarcerating the very people in its community who will slip further into poverty and criminalization because of the loss of services.[35]

And when there are no bodies left nearby, prisons increasingly look beyond their immediate setting to alleviate the mass-warehousing of people elsewhere. States such as California move thousands of prisoners (without any due process) to less crowded private prisons, a simpler solution than facing the profound problem of mass incarceration.[36] The fallout from this interstate trafficking of prisoners is the citizen version of family separation—further destruction of the detainee's family; erosion of communities; limited access to counsel; and an assurance of continued recidivism (aside from the multitude of other abuses that take place in prison every day).[37]

Not unlike the migrant bodies upon which it built an empire, the industry will keep clawing in all sorts of others, including those citizen bodies left destitute by capitalism. Despite the political dividing lines put up between migrant and citizen, they can easily be shifted for the sake of profit. The two groups possess a common link of suffering and oppression, in this case, very real, shared chains.

Much like the profit motive that increasingly is indifferent to the bodies it warehouses, the arm of sovereign power has begun pushing at the edges of the protections extended to citizens. As defense attorney Isabel Garcia notes about Streamline—the move from civil deportation to criminalization "has normalized [the] disregard of formal procedural requirements in our criminal courts..." Streamline Magistrate Judge Velasco echoes:

> What we are willing to do to ourselves in the name of criminal justice is horrible, and Streamline is not an exception. Think about the debtors' prisons we're creating for economically stressed American citizens. Is this what we really want to do? The saving grace of Streamline—if there is one—is that we are just doing to others what we already do to ourselves.[38]

The arm of power and the indifference to process is increasingly blurring the lines between migrant and citizen outside of the detention system. In 2018, Border Patrol arrested Scott Warren, an Arizona school teacher and member of the humanitarian group No More Deaths, a few hours after the organization posted a video of Border Patrol pouring out jugs of water that No More Deaths had placed in the desert for intending migrants.[39] Warren was prosecuted on three felony charges of conspiracy to transport undocumented immigrants and harboring (laws designed for and normally applied to actual human traffickers).[40] While the prosecution attempted to paint him as a human smuggler, he—out of the 361 human smuggling cases in 2018— was the only defendant they accused of doing so without a profit motive.[41] Natalie Hoffman, Oona Holcomb, Madeline Huse, and Zaachila Orozco McCormick were all convicted on offenses including entering a national wildlife refuge without a permit, abandoning property therein, and operating a motor vehicle in a wilderness area in 2019.[42] This criminalization of humanitarian aid for migrants is part of a growing trend, after then-Attorney General Jeff Sessions ordered federal prosecutors to target "harboring" cases.[43] In Texas, four-time elected city and county attorney Teresa Todd was arrested by CBP and faces investigation for human smuggling after she stopped to help three migrants (one near-death) on the side of the road in 2019.[44]

The justifications for these arrests and convictions reek of the same speciousness that has so often justified the state's use of mass detention—just "enforcing the law."[45] These prosecutions also demonstrate the fragility of a citizen's protection against the dehumanizing forces of capitalism. The fact that rendering aid, saving people from death, or leaving water in the desert can be so easily criminalized exposes not only the empty claim of democracy's supposed hold on sovereign power, but also how quickly the lines of political protection can be re-shaped. As one legal scholar puts it—"[O]ur treatment of aliens ultimately becomes a tale about *us*..."[46] In the mix of capital and power, it is not just political personhood at stake for a few migrants and their allies, but the very means of preserving and protecting the humanity of all.

Chapter 10

Immigration Court

Arely had a remarkably similar case to Sara (from Chapter 1). She too had fled brutal domestic violence at the hands of her husband.[1] The police in El Salvador had done nothing to protect her and out of desperation, she fled the country for the US. Like Sara, she fought her asylum case against a particularly hostile immigration judge. But unlike Sara, she lost, despite having the same clear legal precedent in her favor.

On appeal to the BIA, she won a unanimous verdict, and the case was sent to the immigration judge to complete the required background checks and grant Arely asylum. The immigration judge outright refused to grant Arely asylum and was trying to send the case back to the BIA because he disagreed with the decision. Before the BIA picked up the case again to issue the grant of asylum directly, then-Attorney General Sessions used a rarely deployed power and certified the case to himself. In the infamous *Matter of A-B-*, the Attorney General not only stripped Arely of her right to asylum but used her case to destroy the legal precedent for asylum claims based on domestic violence.

This chapter explores the material reality that informs a supposedly impartial immigration judiciary and picks up the discussion of due process and the rule of law from the previous chapter through the lens of the US asylum system and the Executive Office of Immigration Review. The dividing lines between Sara's protection and Arely's rejection expose not only the system's deep partiality, but ultimately, the brokenness of the rule of law itself.

The exclusive nature of asylum

In order to qualify for asylum one must meet the definition

of a refugee—someone who can demonstrate persecution or a well-founded fear of it based on her race, religion, nationality, membership of a particular social group, or political affiliation.[2] While this language appears plain on its face, its applicability has been the subject of extensive litigation, especially around who qualifies as a member of a particular social group.

There are several "procedural" limitations as well—the applicant must file within a year of arriving in the US and can be removed to a "safe third country" at the discretion of the Attorney General, without any judicial review.[3] The decision of then-Attorney General Jeff Session's to deny women like Arely, fleeing domestic violence, on the basis of a "particular social group," overturned a hard-fought legal precedent to protect these very women.[4] Overnight, the ability to receive protection flipped, and suddenly hundreds, possibly thousands, of similarly-situated asylum seekers could be denied both in immigration courts and at the border.

As written, the requirements for asylum, true to the sovereign power that gives them the space to operate, are about exclusion rather than inclusion. The law possesses a narrowness on both its ends that requires a specialized sort of human suffering to receive protection. On the one hand, if a migrant can show that he was harmed severely enough to rise to the level of persecution (or that he would be if returned to his country), but this harm was not connected to one of the above-listed categories, no asylum.

For example, many children fleeing Central American gang violence and conscription are not entitled to asylum as they do not belong to a particular social group, i.e., a group with immutable characteristic(s) that sets them apart.[5] On the other hand, even if their status as children would be particular enough, the fact that many people suffer awful things at the hands of gangs is sufficient reason to deny the claim, since it muddies the connection between the violence and the group (i.e., widespread gang violence is not particular to them).[6] Thus most asylees can be denied because they are either part of a group that is too specific or not specific enough.

The foundation for asylum's exclusionary nature is more apparent when placed in the context of its origins. From the earliest days of international refugee policy, the US sought to restrict the scope of international refugee protections and focused on Communist countries in a bid to undermine their stability.[7] Indeed, despite the appearance of benevolence, US asylum policy has always been dominated by material interests over human rights.[8] During the Cold War, the US viewed Cubans as refugees but did not see Haitians, then under a series of brutal—but anti-communist—dictators, as victims of persecution.[9] Studies have also concluded that economic interests influence grant rates more than the actual condition of human rights in a country, with "economic" migrants facing higher rejection.[10]

It was not until the passage of the Refugee Act in 1980 that the actual face of the law was modeled after the UN's definition of a refugee, at least facially free of Cold War ideology.[11] Undeterred, the Reagan administration simply recast the thousands of Salvadorans and Guatemalans fleeing human rights violations from governments backed by the US as "economic" migrants.[12] Compared to the 40 percent approval rate for Afghans fleeing the Soviet invasion, Salvadorans and Guatemalans were approved at under 3 percent in 1984.[13] This trajectory is born out in recent data—asylum seekers from China are granted asylum at a rate of nearly 80 percent while those from Mexico at only 12 percent.[14] In short, ideology, not a human-rights centered legal analysis, drives asylum outcomes.[15] This is obviously true in Arely's case. Despite the legal precedent, the instability in the wake of the 2008 crash, together with the changing of the guard within the ruling class, gave way to the current tide of nationalism and economic woes that shaped immigration policy accordingly, even within the judiciary.

Even momentarily presuming the law's facial fairness as to

the kinds of people who should be granted asylum, immigration judges (commonly referred to as IJs)—the "linchpin[s]" of US asylum policy,[16]—reveal how far the gap truly is between the ideal of the law and its application. Within individual judicial decisions, the primary driver of asylum grants is neither fact nor law, but the identity of the immigration judge assigned to the case (as is abundantly evident in Arely's case).[17] This is not merely an issue between liberal and conservative parts of the country. In San Francisco alone, the odds of denial varied from 9.4 percent *all the way up to 97.1 percent*, depending on the judge.[18] Nor can this be attributed to the quality or merit of the cases coming before the judge—cases are assigned amongst judges on a random basis, sometimes before an asylum application is even filed, and thus, the massive differences between judges do not rest on the actual nature of the cases themselves.[19]

What drives these wide disparities is a question of ideology, which also makes eliminating the gap nearly impossible. Banks Miller and colleagues, after surveying the data surrounding asylum decisions, note—"the causes of variation are too deeply embedded and the contexts in which decisions are made are too varied and influential."[20] The ideologies that drive IJs (wherever they land on the political spectrum) do not reside in legal factors but rather in things wholly outside the four corners of the law—material conditions and security concerns.[21] Miller notes—"As scholars of the Supreme Court have long known, attitudinal preferences are like water—they find a way into the decision-making process."[22] In the asylum context, IJs are not only susceptible to the material realities that they are supposed to be above but are the continuation of asylum's exclusionary function painted over with the robe of due process. With dire consequences. Asylum proceedings, as the head of the National Association of Immigration Judges noted, are the equivalent of trying death-penalty cases in a traffic court setting.[23]

Even the existence of judges who do have high grant rates is not evidence of a functional system or even its true possibility. Their existence perpetuates the idea that if all judges were like them, *then* the system would be fair—part of a larger mythology that the law and those who administer it stand in a place of justness from which they distribute equally justifiable outcomes to all people. Arely's arbitrary treatment and the absurd disparity of asylum outcomes is the site of the very breakdown of the concept of the rule of law.

For all of the history and intended pursuit of "equality before the law," the law and the judiciary are no less susceptible to economic and political realities that surround it. As Marx noted long ago, the law and the forms of state power that both interpret and enforce it ultimately "have their roots in the material conditions of life."[24] It is these conditions under capitalism—not the application of true justice—that occupy the space between a migrant's relative safety under the law or her exclusion from it altogether.

The arbitrary rule of law

This gap is further apparent in the brokenness of the present conception of due process. While legal scholars have spilled a great deal of ink on the shades of nuance implied by due process, its central tenant is that procedures and protections exist to hold all to the same principles of fairness and justice. It is key to a conception of the ideal rule of law. Legal scholar Michael Mandel posits that the ideal versus the actual use of due process is best thought of as two opposing notions—one democratic and the other juridical.[25] The democratic sense is one that constrains state power, requiring its accountability to the populace it is supposed to serve; as opposed to the juridical sense, which stresses administrative procedure to reinforce the status quo.[26] Given the present material conditions of capitalism, the rule of law and due process fall into the latter. They are methods of protecting class relations.

As Glenn Greenwald argues in *With Liberty and Justice for Some*, it is precisely the availability of this sort of empty due process that makes economic inequality justifiable to the masses.[27] Despite America's aggrandizement of the founders' conception of equality before the law, many of them, like Jefferson, believed that class positions were not only fair, but essential.[28] Due process is not a democratic force constraining state power and ensuring a level playing field for the many, but ultimately part of the same apparatus that protects economic and political relations for the benefit of a few.

This reduction of the rule of law to the juridical—to process and procedure rather than true accountability—is necessary to protect capitalism from its own failure to address the growing economic oppression and alienation of working people.[29] As Mandel argues, the present rule of law and the judiciary are a form of "legalized" politics, a way "to domesticate class struggle."[30] The rule of law as applied to migrant and citizen is a means for those in power of passing on the first question of economic and political justice—questions of *who* decides what is fair and just—in order to protect the status quo of social relations, albeit through carefully worded opinions.

In Arely's case and that of countless others, the rule of law and the shallow availability of due process is a means of justifying the system's barbaric treatment of them; a way of curtailing democratic participation and their ability to make true demands of justice. Case after case, denial after denial, IJs—whether gladly or reluctantly constrained by the four corners of the law's exclusionary nature—dole out procedure that meets the present juridical and empty notion of due process. They provide the ideal vehicle for claiming that all the requirements of justice are met so long as a migrant's plight has been heard. It legitimizes a notion of justice when the judge nevertheless denies relief and casts an asylee out, often to violence or death.

The demands of justice

The failures of due process and the rule of law are not fundamental failures of equality and fairness, but reflections of a deeper problem of power. Marx long ago recognized that these words can be empty ones—of course the ruling class asserts that the distributions, together with the laws and systems that uphold them, are "fair."[31] This requires a reckoning with the deeper question of *who* is in the position to assert what fair and equal *mean*. For the state and judiciary to function in the present system, they must exist outside and above the law in order to function as that *who*. It is an extension of the same sovereign power that decides who is in and outside the law and allows it to adjudicate what is fair and just.[32] Thus, the "legalization" of the class struggle, the removal of the state from true subjugation and accountability to its populace, is not just a perk of sovereign power, but part of its essence.

Despite its conceptual complexity, this reality is out in the open—the Supreme Court has long recognized sovereign immunity as "an axiom of our jurisprudence. The Government is not liable to suit unless it consents [to it]."[33] This immunity also extends to the elite not necessarily in name, but in form—Greenwald notes the unequal application of justice amongst the classes is nothing new.[34]

While these realities are possibly most evident in how they are deployed against migrants, they are not limited solely to political questions. They are attached to the very means of production. The legalization of the class struggle, its "juridical" nature, are constraints of capitalism itself, a means of placing the private sphere (the means of production) out of democratic reach by protecting the property as conceived under the present economic system. Sovereign power and the immunity that flows from it exist to constrain true economic and political justice under the guise of the "rule of law."

The very concepts of equality, justice, and the rule of law are subservient to the material conditions that give them meaning. They can be easily twisted to justify the injustices of a sovereign power and economic system that are not answerable to the people they allegedly serve. The tragedy of Arely's story, like those of so many other migrants and working-class peoples, lies in this gap between the democratic and juridical, between the power of exclusion and who wields it.

Chapter 11

"Legal" Migration and Citizenship

Jane is a 20-year-old undocumented immigrant.[1] In 2013 she went to the police about a neighbor who repeatedly sexually assaulted her while she was living in the Bronx, New York. She eventually obtained a U-visa certification which is a path to legal status for those that have been helpful in the prosecution of certain crimes. The United States Citizenship and Immigration Services (USCIS) has had her application since 2016 and as of August 2019, has yet to process it. In response to a federal lawsuit by her attorney, the government argued in its motion to dismiss that there is no reason to prioritize certain U-visa applications over others and the wait time is no more unreasonable than most other petitioners—in essence, that USCIS has no obligation to act.

Jane is part of a backlog of over 250,000 U-visa cases.[2] While there is a limit of 10,000 U-visas annually, approved applications can be put on a waitlist which allows them to remain lawfully in the country and work until a visa is available.[3] The extensive wait for approval, however, increasingly comes with a risk of deportation, as ICE has begun targeting vulnerable immigrants with pending applications.[4] This chapter explores the self-serving myths of the lawful immigration process, the administrative state that controls it, and arbitrariness of citizenship.

The myth of "legal"

There is a long-standing and pervasive myth about legal immigration that often takes the form of "getting in line," i.e., that migrants present without lawful status simply are disinterested in "waiting their turn" or "doing things the right way." As outlined previously, the "lawful" process never has truly carried the best interests or even the humanity of the migrant, nor has it constituted a sound protection against the arbitrary. This remains true albeit better hidden under the guise of a convoluted process that masks the arbitrary in bureaucracy.

There are two main "gatekeepers" for obtaining legal status outside of the adversarial proceedings of immigration court— USCIS (part of DHS) and the State Department. While their responsibilities at times overlap, USCIS primarily governs immigration issues and processes for migrants inside the country, and the State Department those outside (including family visas, refugee processing, etc.). What is important in both instances, is that the path for an intending migrant is not only fraught, but incredibly narrow. There are three main routes: employment, family, and humanitarian relief. Each is subjected to one of the most intricate dances of regulatory law that rivals only the tax code.

For employment, prior chapters already noted how deeply broken and exploitative that system can be even when it "works"; and an invitation to try to expand it will do little other than perpetuate that evil.

For families going through the Department of State, there are but a few qualified family members that are eligible to bring people outside the US into the country. US citizens can petition for their spouses, parents, children, and siblings. Lawful Permanent Residents (green card holders) can petition for spouses and unmarried children. However, visa caps severally restrict the possibilities—while visas are always available for spouses, parents, and minor children of US citizens, the wait for a visa for a Mexican sibling of a US citizen is now over 20 years.[5] In other words, as of the date of this writing, there are visas available for someone who applied for a sibling *in 1997*.

In all instances, this nevertheless requires a family member who has actually succeeded in obtaining status and has both the financial means not only of paying for the process but also has a demonstrable basis for supporting any and all people she petitions for. Even assuming there is a visa and the monetary availability, the intending immigrant faces a plethora of eligibility requirements, and a single misstep (or at times, even a misunderstanding) could result in a denial with little recourse.

The state-side process through USCIS is equally fraught. There is a wild range of average waiting times where migrants and their families are left in limbo. For example, simple processes like replacing a green card average 8 months, those to adjust status to permanent resident 14 months, and the U-visa for victims of crime has a wait of just shy of 4 years.[6] This deep bureaucratic mess is part of a vast regulatory framework that provides USCIS with broad discretion to deny applications altogether with minimal appellate review. Despite its supposed non-adversarial nature, USCIS is increasingly coordinating with ICE to detain people who show up to interviews in the process of trying to fix their status.[7]

These realities have several significant effects on the immigrant-capitalist cycle and destroy the myth of "jumping the line." The treacherous administrative slog not only discourages but outright denies many people from meaningfully accessing the few immigration benefits that might be available to them. This necessarily drives them towards undocumented means of being with their families or sustaining themselves. This, coupled with the restrictive laws that create lengthy, sometimes permanent, bars to fixing a migrant's legal status should she depart the country,[8] guarantee that a significant group of people live and remain outside the borderline of personhood, even while on US soil.

Even for those that might come forward, the fraternizing between USCIS and ICE creates an express danger for the mere attempt to "make things right" with the law. These broken bridges of migration perpetuate the myth of a legitimate process which in turn feeds the idea of "lawbreaking" migrants when they are forced to circumvent it in order to survive, thus reinvigorating the cycle anew. The administrative process is but another means of dehumanizing migrants, reducing their familial bonds, means of living, and very survival to questions of arbitrary "merit" under the facade of a legal process.

The "nature" of naturalization

USCIS's power is most evident in the naturalization process, the last stop for a migrant in a bid to move themselves out from under the dictates of state control. While it offers more protection for the migrant and even the possibility of political participation, naturalization and its accompanying possibility of denaturalization expose the true arbitrary nature of citizenship, devoid of democratic justification, and revelatory of the profound brokenness of capitalism's logic in sorting people.

Citizenship is the most basic platform upon which people construct the availability of human rights of those belonging to a nation. But it also presents a paradox—on the one hand, it presents the supposedly equal and non-arbitrary basis for protecting and enforcing rights, while on the other, necessarily leaving people out of that circle in order to distinguish who merits those rights. It effectively discriminates on an arbitrary dividing line of the circumstances of one's birth.

The sovereign power whose legitimacy is simply taken for granted rests in its ability to decide who is citizen, to decide when to suspend these basic rights, and in doing so, places itself above the law in order to provide the "rule of law."[9] The citizen is simply someone who falls within the limited protections of the legal order but necessarily at the expense of the lives outside of that same order. The concept of citizenship in the US is as grounded in who it *excludes* as those it includes.

In the context of naturalization, the exclusionary and arbitrary nature of citizenship is evident in the application and citizenship test. The application includes dozens of questions, some of them ludicrous, such as "Have you EVER committed, assisted in committing, or attempted to commit, a crime or offense for which you were NOT arrested?"[10] This paradoxical question is a testament to its design centering around the idea of exclusion rather than inclusion—one must forgo basic rights like the one against self-incrimination in the hope of obtaining that right in its fullest sense after bureaucratic scrutiny.

The citizenship test is equally exclusive by design. With a few narrow exceptions, it requires English proficiency; what USCIS has determined to be important questions regarding US civics and history; and the migrant's assurance that he is "attached" to the principles of the Constitution and form of government. Of course, these requirements are entirely arbitrary—there is no "official" US language; even assuming that the history questions present an accurate portrayal of America's past, a majority of US-born citizens likely cannot pass it;[11] the concept of "attachment" taken to its logical conclusion requires the migrant to agree to either the Constitution as written (regardless of its justness) or some vague notion of certain "principles" that are not articulated and in any case are not required of any natural-born citizen.

These requirements are often defended as necessary to achieve proper civic participation from migrants or assurance of their adequateness to enter political life. Citizenship is constrained not by democratic ideals of who should participate as people fully endowed with rights in American society, but rather is an exercise of the state's authority to dictate who is a "good" citizen.[12] This has taken on different faces: from the earliest statutes allowing only "free white men" to naturalize (and a protracted judicial exploration of who was "not white" without ever establishing who was[13]), to actively targeting naturalized political dissidents, to the stripping of Americans of Japanese descent of citizenship, as well as women who married non-citizen men.[14] The present requirements are a further entrenchment of the capitalist notion of meritocracy where people "deserve" their place in society.

But stepping back, even a few paces, is to recognize how

deeply problematic these hurdles are to democracy. Would all US-born citizens agree to parameters that measure their English literacy, or their understanding of a one-sided view of history, or the exploration of any possible wrongdoing in their past (convicted or not) as the basis for whether they possess rights? Unlikely. Rather than its supposed measure of a migrant's merit, the naturalization process is a way of dodging the fundamental first questions of *who* decides who is imbued with inalienable rights and *how* that process is achieved. This unquestioned ability of the capitalist nation-state to dictate the citizen/other dichotomy is a robust exercise of sovereign power, one over migrants and citizens alike rather than the other way around.

This power is equally evident in the state's ability to strip citizenship. Despite the Fourteenth Amendment's citizenship clause — "born or naturalized in the United States" — presenting each type of citizen as equal, this is ultimately a contradictory phrase. For the state to retain and reproduce its sovereign power over an entire populace it must necessarily be able to not only determine who has rights but also possess the ability to take them away.

Under the current statutory scheme, denaturalization generally falls into either a civil context where the migrant obtained citizenship through "concealment of a material fact or will misrepresentation"/was not eligible for naturalization in the first place; or criminal, where the migrant "knowingly procured citizenship unlawfully."[15] The former has no statute of limitations and leaves the migrant forever vulnerable to any possible inconsistency (including responses to the absurd question noted above) as well as the ability to second-guess the arbitrary discretion around the migrant's "good moral character" (in a 2019 report, this provision was cited in nearly all civil denaturalization cases).[16] In the criminal instances, upon conviction, judges can order a defendant's immediate and automatic removal from the US.[17]

The power to denaturalize, despite its language around targeting "bad" migrants (at this point in America's history courts have limited citizenship-stripping to migrants), serves a much broader political purpose. It is a question of a racialized and arbitrary process of targeting certain foreign-born groups as part of a political agenda to ensure migrant vulnerability and inability to demand proper justification for their treatment.[18] It is, as Masha Gessen notes, a means of "taking away their assumption of permanence,"[19] which, given the nature of sovereign power, was never actually a safe assumption to begin with. The denaturalization process is a post-hoc legitimization of capitalism's arbitrary power to divide people, a way of applying "the law" to validate a fundamentally unjustified process. The migrant can never uncouple herself from her own commodification, its history, and its connection to state power and that power's ability to exclude her from basic rights.

Taken together, the naturalization and denaturalization processes elucidate a disturbing truth. Much like the capitalist system from which modern state sovereignty emerges, at their heart is not the pursuit of a justifiable process towards all participants, but rather, they exist as a means of maintaining and perpetuating power in the hands of a few. To extend the full guarantees of liberty, equality, and justice to all without exception would require sovereign (and capitalism's) power to cede the very thing that guarantees its own control—the ability to dictate the terms of political participation of the many for the sake of the few. Citizens, through the state's physical and political exclusion of migrants, are made to believe time and time again that what separates Americans from non-Americans are issues of merit and justness. In reality, it masks the fragility of everyone's rights as citizens, ones not fully within their grasp.

The nature of administrative power

This gap between the people and those who wield power is also evident within USCIS as part of the greater "administrative state" that, as the Supreme Court noted, has become "a veritable fourth branch of the Government."[20] Increasingly, the limited democratic means that most people have of influencing public policy through the legislature (which is close to nil for most migrants) is even further afield than ever. Those in power have done so through delegation of authority to administrative agencies like USCIS to work out the details of how a particular law is construed and applied, with little judicial oversight. This administrative state plays a significant role in shaping Americans' daily lives under capitalism.

The same power of some administrative agencies that has grown in response to rapid changes in technology (such as drugs and the FDA or Wall Street and the FTC) has also empowered USCIS to issue new rules through the perfunctory "notice-and-comment" process that may have profound impacts on how the law is applied. Or USCIS may issue policy guidance that forgoes the process altogether. In either case, there is little recourse — the Supreme Court has long applied the controversial *Chevron* standard to this agency power which generally affords a great deal of deference to agency ruling-making and decisions.[21] In USCIS's case, this administrative power allows it to shape the rules towards dictating the flow of lawful migrants (often in response to other shifts in economic and political power[22]) rather than pursuing a universal ideal of "fairness."

The administrative state's origins were primarily just ones, a pursuit, as one scholar notes of "substantive aspirations to counteract inequalities, hierarchies, and disparities of power generated by a changing social and economic order" in early industrial America.[23] The administrative state, at least in part, was an attempt to democratize the accountability of private economic actors whose market power necessarily threatened the rest of the public's political power.[24]

But like so many other hard-fought working-class victories during the New Deal era, in the intervening years, it has faced a slow and persistent hijacking back towards ruling-class dominance by the forces of privatization and centralization.[25] Privatization, on the one hand, is a systematic dismantling of public service by special (capitalist) interests, (like private prisons); this not only neuters the agency's power but directs what power it has towards the interests of the few.[26] Centralization, on the other hand, is consolidating the bureaucratic power of the agencies (like USCIS) that can "run roughshod over the need to engage stakeholders in participation, imbuing its responsibilities with overly political or ideological motivations..."[27]

Thus, immigrants and their advocates are caught in a kind of double-blackmail where the pursuit of the destruction of the administrative state will serve to enhance corporate and ruling-class power in one arena, while enhancement of bureaucratic power to restrict the ravages of capitalism will be leveraged against migrants in another. These two forces share a common purpose: "preventing the deploying of state power to dismantle structural economic and social inequalities."[28]

It is ultimately a false dichotomy to argue strictly for or against the administrative state rather than recognizing what such power actually reveals about citizen and migrant's collective relationship to it. The bigger question than the "benefit" or the danger of administrative authority is one of its accountability, as it is a microcosm of everyone's relationship to the state writ large.

The administrative state, and maybe especially USCIS, offers a window into exactly how broken America's supposed democracy is—immigration policy, and a host of other things affecting the working class, is largely shaped by a procedure out of the reach of those most affected by it. It is an age-old question, one not of whether there is something inherently "good" or "bad" about the (administrative) state, but whether those most affected by its choices can demand true participation in the pursuit of collectively justifiable means of economic and political organization. It is a question as to whether the "coercive tools of the state are in fact deployed towards publicly legitimate—and contestable, and nonarbitrary—ends."[29]

Chapter 12

The Failures of Reform

Regardless of one's political stripes—the brokenness of the immigration system is a source of consistent agreement. What needs to be remedied, however, is not. This chapter explores the traditional avenues of change—enforcement, politics, the judiciary or other institutions—and ultimately why they are unable to bridge the gap between migrants and the possibility of a just and equitable system.

Protectionism will not repair anything

Numerous analysts, think-thanks, and commentators, even conservative ones, have rightly noted the harm the system does to immigrants and their American working-class counterparts. Often their solutions revolve around protectionism, a reduction in migrant flows, and ignore the greater problem within capitalism itself.

Setting aside the obvious and likely humanitarian atrocities of aggressive enforcement if ICE and CBP had open license against undocumented people, the economic impact in America alone would be catastrophic—the costs to remove most undocumented workers and prevent future entry have estimates of $500 to $600 billion; together with the damage to GDP, a potential drop of $1.6 trillion over 20 years due to the loss of migrant labor.[1] The system would suffer a substantial loss of tax income—PNAE estimates that undocumented immigrants paid $15.9 billion in federal taxes in 2016;[2] the Institute on Taxation & Economic Policy estimates that immigrants pay $11.74 billion in state and local taxes each year at an estimated 8 percent of their income, versus the top 1 percent of taxpayers rate of 5.4 percent.[3] Taxes that are not likely to be made up by that same 1 percent. Even social programs would suffer—the Social Security Administration estimates that unauthorized workers pay billions each year that they will never be able to draw on.[4] American capitalism (even the social protections therein) literally cannot afford to go on without exploiting immigrants. This is not to say that migrant exploitation should continue in order to prop-up ailing social programs but rather to establish that migrants allow capitalists to have their cake and eat it too.

The protectionist approach, including that advocated by some on the left,[5] leaves intact the relationship between classes and property rights that reduces migrants—and all workers—to something less than human. It takes for granted that the divisions between people set out by and for capitalism are legitimate. Arguing for fair treatment of all workers is quite different from ensuring that the citizen workers are treated marginally better through immigration controls. Working-class suffering, migrant or citizen, will not be remedied by such short-sighted thinking. As Marx argued when discussing the hostilities between English and immigrant Irish working classes in his day—this antagonism only serves the capitalist class, "It is the secret by which [it] maintains its power."[6] Protectionism ultimately fosters the very problem it is trying to solve: pitting working-class people against one another, making the union of working classes impossible.[7]

Protectionism also incorrectly assumes that given a reduction of immigrants within the US, the oppression and exploitation of the American working class will improve, rather than realizing that the capitalists will simply have to find other means of reducing labor costs either by outsourcing or automating labor. The resolution does not lie in reducing the number of working bodies in the US, but in challenging the control of those bodies as commodities and the system of organizing labor and rights that perpetuates such dehumanization. Capitalism dictates an endless pursuit of reducing labor costs without regard to the laborer. Capitalism will forever require pitting citizens and migrants against each other; forever require a revisiting of new and creative ways of exploitation; and forever require power over who is in and out based not on humanitarian, universal ideals but questions of profit. Protectionism will protect no one but the capitalists.

No help is coming

America's institutions are unlikely to bring about deep change. The answer will not come from the judiciary. There remains an age-old legal doctrine of the state's nearly unbridled power over immigrants. There is nothing within the rule of law in its current configuration that will guarantee against racist and xenophobic policies, much less a fundamental repositioning of migrants under the full protection of the law (which is itself a fragile line). The legal implementation of the "Muslim Ban" as well as the ability to force asylum seekers to apply from Mexico are samples of recent proof that the judiciary has tied its hands on central questions of sovereign power and how it is wielded.

The administrative state, so long as it remains democratically unaccountable to all, will at best trade hands between slightly better humanitarian approaches—like Deferred Action for Childhood Arrivals (DACA)—or become an extension of the enforcement arm—like USCIS turning undocumented people over to ICE who are attempting to fix their status. There will be no way of tinkering with regulatory reforms towards the end of migrant oppression from a system that can turn on a dime against those abandoned outside of the political order. The task of deep change to remedy the divide between migrants and their humanity within the system cannot be left to bureaucrats to reform. Even if the immigration benefits and admissibility were extensively opened, their permissive nature (including asylum), renders both them and the law that creates them devoid of true justice.

Similarly, the international stage offers little protection. One of the only protections against facially ethnic-based immigration policies is the system of independent nation-states throughout the world.[8] This is rooted in the idea that each state is a representative of its people and therefore acts of discrimination against its nationals in a foreign country are a diplomatic no-no.[9] Yet, UN conventions and treaties have left large concessions open on the issue of how each nation controls immigrant admissions, separate and apart from the unlikelihood of enforcement of agreed-upon norms.[10] More importantly, the conception of fairness between the peoples of respective nations presupposes several fallacies as truths — that nation-states actually represent the interests of even a majority of their population rather than the elite that so often control them and that all nation-states are viewed and treated as equals.

To leave progress of migrant treatment in the hands of those in power in the judiciary, international community, or the administrative state is to continue the age-old game of ignoring the humanitarian realities that confront the planet in favor of using migrants as political and economic pawns.

Neo-Liberalism has failed

Nor can neo-liberal politics be trusted to re-frame the nature of migration, even the Democratic Party. As Professor Suzy Lee details — "on the questions of migration quotas, economic migration, or border enforcement, the Democratic Party has always been restrictionist. It has simply insisted that the policy be tempered by humanitarian concerns such as the reunification of families and the extension of rights to unauthorized immigrants who are already in the country."[11]

This is most apparent in the end of DACA and its unimplemented extension for certain migrant parents known as Deferred Action for Parents of Americans (DAPA). President Obama implemented DACA as a means of giving undocumented children a form of legal-adjacent status, able to apply for work permits, attend college, and receive marginal protection against ICE and deportation. The eligible population included about 1.3 million and about 800,000 had received DACA when President Trump decided to end the program.[12] DAPA never even got off the ground. While many immigration practitioners initially saw DACA as a positive, humanizing moment, what became apparent is that this kind of shallow bureaucratic reform is exactly the sort that can be abused at the changing of the guard. Those 800,000 not only face losing jobs and the means of narrow protections, but have handed over a great deal of identifying information to an agency that increasingly collaborates with ICE. DACA in many ways was an opening of the door just wide enough to slam it on the people who started to come inside.

While DACA undoubtedly allowed some migrants a degree of respite and for a few more, a means of permanent status (through an intricate weave of legal maneuvering with qualifying US relatives), it was a moralizing patchwork that ultimately did little more than demand that some migrants be treated "nicer"; a kind of political rebuke to the conservative wing of the government for being so callous towards these migrants brought over as children. It did not face the fundamental injustice rooted in the immigration system and the status quo it protects. This kind of moralizing poses a deeper problem—it can be readily spun around against migrants, as white supremacists like Coleman Blease did nearly a century ago which resulted in their criminalization.

The Democratic Party's moralizing is a failure not because migrants are undeserving of empathy, but because it serves only as a smokescreen to hide the party's true restrictionist nature. The party believes it cannot be both on the side of the citizen and migrant working class. Instead it attempts to develop an acceptable moral framework to treat migrants "fairly" within the confines of capitalism while appeasing the hurt of the American citizen worker through other restrictionist means.

As an example, even as Obama promoted DACA and its moral justness, his administration deported 2.5 million— more people than the *sum deported by all of the twentieth century's presidents*.[13]

On the other hand, the party's response to xenophobia and nativism looks to blame the white working class for their role in migrant suffering—that because the nativists possess largely unfounded cultural and economic anxieties (making them easy targets for capitalist manipulation), they are the primary obstacle to migrant liberation rather than the material conditions that have fostered intra-class conflict in the first place.

This two-faced approach is doomed to fail because it is grounded in reaction and never moves above the irreconcilable contradiction of a "fair" distinction between citizen and migrant within capitalism. As Grandin notes—the lesson taught by the history of US involvement in Latin America is "[d]emocracy, social and economic justice, and political liberalization have never been achieved through an embrace of empire but rather through resistance to its command."[14] To attempt a balancing act of rights and restrictions is to guarantee migrant suffering into the future at the expense of true democracy and justice.

None of this is to say that the efforts to bring migrants into legal safety, organize them under the current system, or combat racism are in vain; every move made to secure them with protections against the capitalist state is a small step closer to ending their oppression. Even within the broken American immigration system, migrants and their children are slowly gaining a majority within the citizenship and have the potential to make shifts within the current framework. However, for the same reasons that reformist tinkering is insufficient, this is not cause to celebrate. A shift in the population does not guarantee future migrant rights. This should be apparent from the example of the once ostracized and "non-white" Irish migrants. So long as the material conditions that give rise to xenophobia and racism remain in place, there is the possibility of their rebirth over and over, no matter how many of Hydra's heads are cut off. Leaving sovereign power in the hands of a few to condition a person's political existence and rights will always subvert any movement to fully humanize migrants and bring about the necessary cross-border solidarity. The material conditions of existence— capitalism—will always have the last word.

The disconnect of universal rights

Even pleas to a truly universal conception of human rights are fraught. While the arbitrary and often oppressive legal division of people should result in its wholesale rejection, it is insufficient to simply argue that immigrants are "like" everyone else and therefore should be afforded the same fundamental rights assumed by the Constitution or the notion of equality in the Declaration of Independence.

It is precisely because of the inconsistent adherence to and application of universal ideals that racial and legal divides emerged. Ones that came to be seen as natural and that justified capitalist relations and the dehumanization of entire groups. This calls for a solution beyond the "more humane" treatment of migrants. As refugee and scholar Hannah Arendt noted in *The Origins of Totalitarianism*, human rights are least effective when they are most needed, as one can only acquire them by being part of a political community, such as the nation-state.[15] Refugees are devoid of these rights because they have been cast out from the political community they were once a part of.

Because rights are not some metaphysical thing existing outside of human interactions or the material conditions that set the table for those interactions, there is a desperate need for a new, radically democratic reimagining of rights. This cannot be conceived in a vacuum, there is not a metaphysical set of rights existing independent of people interacting with one another. Rather, they are grounded in material reality and must be addressed there. As Luxemburg argued—"Social Democracy does not demand a declaration of [an] imaginary 'right' on the basis of the existing system, but rather strives for the abolition of the system itself by class struggle."[16]

Thus, what is required is not just a resistance to the methods of oppression or conception of migrants as nonpersons, but a struggle for equality that targets the fundamental structure that makes both possible. Capitalism's control over migrant bodies persists in part because citizens have not broken free of its control over *their own*.

This concession to capitalism, allowing it to define "us" and "them," does not protect or further life, liberty, and the pursuit of happiness for the many but the power of a few. In their present form, neither national ideas nor the Constitution will undo the broken nature of citizenship and rights. So long as nations and nation-states reflect an arbitrary method of ruling-class "self-determination," they can never be a vehicle for worker (or migrant) liberation.[17]

The crisis of humanitarian migration has always revealed the inadequacy of pleas to human universality, since sovereign power and the nature of citizenship are built upon who is excluded. It is here, at the borderlines drawn by capital, that the fight for this new conception must be waged and won. It is not for the sake of the migrant alone. As Malik writes—so long as "we allow states to detain, abuse and bar migrants on the grounds that they are not citizens...we not only deny others their rights; we expose the fragility of our rights, too."[18] The true challenge is not the opening of borders, but what lies beyond them—a conception of human rights that arises out of something other than nation-states and the economic system that produced them.

Chapter 13

Erasing the Borderlines

What solutions remain? The brokenness of the immigration system and the very ideas of American democracy and justice reveal that the answer does not and cannot lie within the bounds of capitalism. The forces and structures that benefit from cheap migrant bodies to perpetuate both profit and power will not be toppled by reformist tinkering, which, at best, attempts to allow a few more immigrants into the political body.

Nor will the ravages of global capitalism be undone by a more "orderly" attempt at controlling migration. An attempt at orderly control or small advancements in humanizing treatment are fundamentally at odds with how sovereign power is exercised in the modern era—it is not a question of "how could anyone do this to people" but instead of "how can people be reduced that such treatment is permissible."[1] Positing the question in this light requires more than a moral struggle against what is happening to human beings (because neither their oppressors nor the system see them as such) but rather requires confronting the dehumanizing totality that justifies and demands such treatment.

Democratic reordering and a true picture of justice

The struggle to humanize migrants and reclaim true democracy is a collective fight for more than momentary economic or political security. It is a radical reordering of the social and political world in favor of a new, fundamentally democratic means of organizing labor and with it, a shared humanity. The answer lies in the demand for a democratic justification of the borderlines that capitalism has used to split people from economic, political, and humane justice.

The struggle to realize true democracy and a set of universal human rights will continue to consistently collide against the reality that it is only through the current arrangement of nation-states that anyone possesses rights at all.[2] Arendt's limited solution was to create a supranational law that consists of only one right: to belong to a political community—the right to have rights.[3] However, Arendt was deeply skeptical that humanity, in its current arrangement of nation-states, could deliver this right, as it would have to transcend the current conception of international law and nations themselves.[4]

The beginnings of a resolution to this problem demand a different conception of rights, which is tied to the question of what is just. It requires something more than mere formalized procedures for determining who resides inside and outside the borders of political life or of what true democracy must look like. Justice requires, as philosopher and theorist Rainer Forst argues—that one have the moral right to reject arbitrariness and domination within the social and political order.[5] It is a conception of democracy as not merely electoral politics and shallow republicanism, but fundamentally rooted in the ability to put justice into practice.[6] Forst calls this the fundamental *right to justification*.[7]

In an international context, he argues that this right precedes all other demands for human rights.[8] It is the most basic claim of each person to be respected as an end in itself and cannot be treated in a way that lacks adequate reciprocal and general reasons—in other words, each person may not demand for herself what she denies to others.[9] This right does not arise from some universalist absolute but rather is grounded in the material world, the interactions between people and the claims they make on one another.[10] It is a theoretical development of an age-old maxim—the requirement to treat others as one would be treated. In Forst's conception, democracy requires not just that rules be equally applied to all but that all who are subjected to them are co-authors of them.[11] "[D]emocracy...is not 'instrumental' to justice; *it is what justice demands*"[12] (emphasis mine).

Under this conception of justice and democracy, the present immigration system in the US, together with all of its evils, lacks the most basic foundation of proper justification. Its historically consistent premise—that an elite few should dictate the terms of political protection and participation in America's communities based on the circumstances of one's birth—cannot rise to the challenge of true justice. It is grounded in the deeply flawed justification that each person "belongs" somewhere and, as such, is afforded the necessary political protection of their home nation. But, as noted already, refugees break this very notion of reciprocal political inclusion. Birthplace (and its attendant circumstances), unlike citizenship, is inalienable. Birthplace as a dividing line is neither reciprocal nor general—those that are born "into" citizenship have no more earned their place than those born outside of it. Birthplace, like skin color or sex, cannot form a justifiable basis for political inclusion. Democracy and the right to justification demand more than capitalism's empty and self-serving reasons for the divide between people.

In the current moment, the issue of migration can be narrowed further to the question of free movement, which is tantamount to the right to physical presence in a country. This right, as Professor Lee clarifies, "is a precondition for securing all other rights."[13] As Forst puts it—the right to justification does not end at borders.[14] The lack of reciprocity between the migrant, stateless or not, and the citizen cannot be reconciled in any truly just terms other than political equality between them.

There certainly are circumstances where free movement can and possibly should be reduced. For example, a pandemic or a natural disaster. But in these instances, the restrictions of physical presence must still meet the demands of justice—a requirement for social distancing or isolation during a pandemic must be grounded in mutual protection of peoples and vulnerable populations. This is both reciprocal and general—one can both ask this behavior of others and have the same asked of one's self. Contrast this with the stated and implied justifications of national security, the rule of law, and even the spread of the capitalist conception of democracy. These are all tied to capitalism's sovereign power and control over human movement (and the rights pertaining thereto) that, as discussed throughout, are in service of the status quo of economic and political power in the hands of the few. Thus, the present arrangement of political power fails at the task of true justice, and with it, the possibility of humanizing migrants.

Economic justice and humanization

This dehumanizing nature of sovereign power's exclusion of migrants is shared by the economic system that propels it and is an oppression that knows no borders, as Marx observed:

> The worker becomes all the poorer the more wealth he produces, the more his production increases in power and size. The worker becomes an ever cheaper commodity the more commodities he creates. The devaluation of the world of men is in direct proportion to the increasing value of the world of things. Labor produces not only commodities; it produces itself and the worker as a commodity – and this at the same rate at which it produces commodities in general.[15]

Even as migrant bodies prop-up capitalism's exercise of power and the accumulation of profit, the system drags all workers indiscriminately towards dehumanization.

The prevailing order's justifications for control over migrants and their exclusion from the political body resonate in its justification of control over the means of production— the presumption that capitalism and its market forces, much like the rule of law, have rightly and fairly determined each person's place and drawn the lines accordingly. As James Kwak argues, this unwavering belief—what he terms "economism"—in the capitalist system not only provides a justification for increasingly unequal outcomes, but helps hold the very system together.[16] This ideology removes the question of who gets what from the political sphere, guaranteeing the market's "ideal" solution is protected against collective accountability.[17] It is the interpretative framework of the wealthy few that ensures their preferred political course and the justification against inequality—"By veiling the operation of wealth and power behind symbolic imagery of markets, economism protects the existing order from democratic challenge."[18]

There are many shared sufferings between migrant and citizen, not just in the forms of economic exploitation but also in direct oppression—the prison-industrial complex, the arbitrary deployment of law, the exercise of sovereign power and violence. It exists in the ideologies of racism and xenophobia that arose as justifications to protect power relations. Despite citizens' limited rights and protections, they are increasingly cut off from political power.

Thus, US capitalism, power, and the borders between people meet at this fundamental point of justice. And at this convening of the economic and political, as Forst notes, the question of justice demands more than redistribution, it demands lasting change in production, distribution, and political decision-making.[19] It requires examining the first question of justice—who has power?[20] The supposed institutions that protect American democracy and its citizens are but a means of an elite few maintaining power, one that is out of reach of the laboring masses.

Rejecting the nation-state's self-serving division of citizens and migrants is the beginning of a rejection of the economic and political conditions that make it possible. It is a reorientation towards justice, a necessary working-class union across borders to demand proper justification of the present order. Capitalism has not and cannot deliver true liberty, fraternity, and democracy; only empty promises to a growing body of impoverished people for whom these rights and the American Dream will stay out of reach.

An international movement armed with this right to justification is the only means of confronting these failures. It is precisely in this moment—where capitalism and its exploitative power have spanned the globe; ushered in the threat of catastrophic climate change; helped spur the massive and deadly displacement of human beings—that a global response is needed. A global challenge to a socio-political order that lives not through democratic participation and accountability but the fear of it. Through its global spread, capitalism has accidentally provided the planet with an inkling of the immense power and possibility of shared cooperation (one that can hopefully be freed of coercive and exploitative means).

On the question of power, as Agamben points out, even revolutionary democratic movements must grapple with the issue of sovereign power and its seemingly required bare life.[21] Reorganization of political life still faces the problem of how the law is created and the latent power of violence in its enforcement.[22] Agamben argues that because bare life has been created in the world, it is "no longer confined to a particular place or a definite category. It now dwells in the biological body of every living being."[23] Neither Agamben nor any of his interlocutors have contrived a way beyond this problem.

Yet, there is at least an imperfect progression—if sovereign power cannot be entirely nullified, at minimum, it can at least exist within the right to justification. The fact that both a fascist regime and a deeply democratic one can exercise sovereign power does not make the two equivalents. As Forst argues under the right to justification—"[t]here can therefore be no absolute claim to sovereignty according to which imperatives of sovereignty trump human rights. Rights are not 'granted' vertically by a state, but instead are accepted and conferred horizontally in a process of justification, and thus are an expression of mutual recognition."[24] In both totalitarian and democratic political bodies, justifications are being provided; however, it is only in the latter that they can become adequate.

This does not require the wholesale rejection of the concept of law or its equally applied rule, but rather, as Mandel argues, requires its reorientation towards "a radical democratization of social life."[25] Marx, despite his deep skepticism of the law, nevertheless realized the value of leveraging the law to enshrine political victories like limiting the working-day.[26] For migrant and citizen alike, it is a question of challenging the fundamental justifications underlying not just the legal system and the nature of due process, but the very accessibility of the rule of law, how it is applied, and whose interests it furthers. It is a question of re-focusing justice beyond the narrow confines of ruling-class ideology towards the very basis on which its power rests, of moving beyond the juridical nature of the law towards its positive and robust democratic potential.

Reimagining both immigrants and citizens as being fully endowed with the ability to seize hold of the right to demand justification for the lines others have drawn—between human beings, between qualified and bare life, between worker and the means of production—is a step towards reclaiming the collective humanity ebbing away in the flood of capital.

There will be problems

Even after embracing this ideal of the human right to justification, there are a multitude of problems that might confront the struggle for true democracy, some readily recognized from public discourse—the inability of social systems and other resources to withstand a sudden population increase; further depression of wages; cultural or civic retrogression and the limits of tolerance; nativist backlash; and national security—to name some prominent ones. While not exhaustive, many of the objections fall into one of these categories.

While all of these questions are pragmatic on their face, they do not look beyond the present circumstances dictated by capitalism. They present a false dichotomy—that a borderless society is either workable and affordable or not under the present material circumstances, rather than face the fundamental issue of justice. One may as well ask whether capitalism can afford to turn over the means of production to the working class. The fact that capitalism cannot fulfill the promise of a freer person and answer to foundational claims of what is just is exactly why it must end.

It's apparent that massive monetary redistribution is not a utopian fantasy but a present-day capitalist reality—the bailouts of the mid-2000s handed over hundreds of billions, taken from the working class, to the very capitalists who decimated the economy.[27] Yet, this was only 3.5 percent of US gross domestic product in 2009.[28] The eight richest families in the world control as much wealth as the poorest 50 percent.[29] The richest 1 percent own more wealth than the rest of the planet.[30] The workers of the world are clearly capable of producing massive wealth. A borderless world without want is not a question of sufficient resources—there is more than enough of that, just in private hands. Even assuming a shortage, choices about where resources should be allocated in a mutually cooperative, democratically justified context, requires something that capitalism cannot give. In a justified context, the question of scarcity fundamentally differs—it looks to how each person and the collective can sustain themselves rather than preserve an individual "right" to uncapped accumulation.

In the area of cultural regression, there is little to fear. Setting aside instances of outright racism and xenophobia, consider the hand-waving about the Muslim diaspora and its possible claimed regressive effects on Western values. Pew reports a growing trend of Muslims accepting liberal views in the US, even as the number of Muslim immigrants and overall population grows.[31] As one example, the number of Muslim-Americans who believe that society should accept homosexuality has doubled from 27 percent in 2007 to 52 percent in 2017 and has essentially closed the gap between them and the rest of the US population.[32] In other words, a Muslim-American is no more likely to reject a gay person than any other randomly chosen member of the US population.

The significance of this example abides in its *possibility*. It requires an acceptance of the notion of a human being as something other than a static entity. Even in America's broken capitalist system, people were still able to change in less than a decade. Imagine the possibilities where, free from the constraints of capital, the multitudes work out these problems. By its nature, the right to justification invites all in to both demand and provide an accounting for how they treat others and are treated themselves. The truly radical position is not walling-off in an attempt to "preserve" progressive ideas, but inviting as many people as possible to engage with them in pursuit of a collective justice, free of domination.

This possibility of true justice and democracy necessarily extends to concerns about the backlash of white nationalism or alt-rightism. As should be evident from the rest of the book, these sorts of reaction to migrants are not new. As Pew notes, since the early days of refugee admissions, the American populace has largely opposed their entrance to the country.[33] To allow these voices to dictate the terms of basic human rights is to allow racism and xenophobia—ugly extensions of capitalism— to undermine basic justice. Unions once demanded that women be kept out of the workplace, both because of sexist traditional views of women as lesser people and the potential that capitalists would use them to suppress wages.[34] The US once enslaved black bodies, then demanded their separation from white ones, and now incarcerates them in disproportionate numbers. The Irish weren't always "white."

Despite the persistence of racism and xenophobia, the response, both then and now, is to gather up the strength of the working class, to seek unity against a common threat that seeks to divide and dominate. This movement towards solidarity with migrants necessarily also takes up the problems of sexism, racism, and xenophobia—addressing the problems of economic exploitation in a collective fashion requires parallel pursuits of justice and equality in all other areas. These ugly institutions have been built by human hands and minds and can be torn down in the same manner. A proper context of justice and democratic participation can create the space in which, in a post-capitalist world, all people dialogue and struggle for understanding and acceptance, a true freedom that is not beholden to the domination of capital. Restricting movement and migrants' humanity based on the sensibilities of the capitalist system will not end working-class suffering and exploitation in America, nor will it make people safer.

The erosion of the capitalist order will also necessarily launch inquiries into new horizons of progress. While no one can foresee all possibilities or consequences, a radical reorganization of the material and relational boundaries between people will require fundamental changes to long-standing social orders. The same justificatory demands for capitalism's division between people can be extended to the hierarchies within those same people.

All problems are soluble

There is a superseding argument to these many objections—the fact that problems may endure is not enough to continue this systemic dehumanization of migrants. Much like the end of slavery required a radical rethinking of an entire population's place in society and in no way immediately abated long-standing tensions or the suffering of people of color. America is still wrestling with that trauma as a society, still pursuing an end to the divisions of skin and the pain they carry under capitalism. Yet, the fact that this struggle persists was not and is not a proper justification for perpetuating such an oppressive, inhumane institution a day longer. This requires a rethinking of what is possible. As Forst notes in his conceptualization of global justice—realistic "does not mean within the reach of practical politics; rather, it means in touch with reality."[35] To borrow from author and physicist David Deutsch—problems are inevitable *but they are also soluble.*[36]

The prevailing order cannot justify migrant criminalization, family separation, labor exploitation, or the host of other evils in any terms other than preserving itself. The migrant liberation movement's resolve to resist these evils should be strengthened rather than cowed by the challenges of humanizing migrants. The existence of tensions between the respective members of the working class in the form of wage depression, nativism, and cultural clashes points to the need to confront, in a unified fashion, the material conditions that created and maintain these divisive forces, not shy away from them and continue to hide behind walls.

Reimagining democracy is a question not of its practicality, but its potential to reshape human interaction between citizen, migrant, and the very means of sustaining life itself. A true picture of democracy, one rooted in the right of all people to demand and provide accountability for how each is treated from all others, is the very place where the end of the nightmare that is capitalism can end, and a new, more just political economy can begin. Open borders, the end of capitalism's division between citizen and migrant, and a radical reorganization of labor between people are not just the beginnings of this new democracy—they are the necessary outcomes of the peoples' demand for justice.

References and Endnotes

Chapter 1

1 Throughout the text, some names have been changed.

2 Friedrich Engels, "Socialism: Utopian and Scientific, Part III: Historical Materialism," in *Marx & Engels Selected Works, Volume 3* (Moscow: Progress Publishers, 1970).

Chapter 2

1 Suzy Lee, "The Case for Open Borders," *Catalyst*, vol. 2, Issue 4, (2019), https://catalyst-journal.com/vol2/no4/the-case-for-open-borders.

2 Mary Bilder, "The Struggle over Immigration: Indentured Servants, Slaves, and Articles of Commerce," in Mo. Law Review 61, no. 4 (1996): 749.

3 Ibid., 753.

4 Ibid., 756-7, 761.

5 Ibid., 762.

6 Ibid., 776, 767.

7 Ibid., 769.

8 Ibid., 750, 808.

9 Ibid., 799.

10 Ibid., 807.

11 Ibid., 822-3.

12 Ibid., 824.

13 Edward C. Carter, "A 'Wild Irishman' Under Every Federalist's Bed: Naturalization in Philadelphia, 1789-1806," *The Pennsylvania Magazine of History and Biography* 94, no. 3 (1970): 331-46.

14 David Scott Fitzgerald and David Cook Martin, *Culling the Masses: The Democratic Origins of Racist Immigration Policy in the Americas* (Cambridge: Harvard University Press, 2014), 89.

15 Jon Michael Haynes, "Saying We're Sorry? New Federal Legislation and the Forgotten Promises of the Treaty on Guadalupe Hidalgo, *Scholar: St. Mary's Law Review on Minority Issues* 3 (2001): 231.

16 Fitzgerald, *Culling the Masses*, 101.

17 Ibid.

18 John Burnett, "The Bath Riots: Indignity Along the Mexican Border," *NPR*, January 28, 2006, https://www.npr.org/templates/story/story. php?storyId=5176177. The practice of fumigating Mexican laborers continued for decades.

19 US Congress, House of Rep., Committee on Immigration and Naturalization, *Seasonal agricultural laborers from Mexico: Hearings Committee on Immigration and Naturalization*, 69th Congress, 1926, 6.

20 Natalia Molina, *How Race is Made in America: Immigration Citizenship, and the Historical Power of Racial Scripts* (Berkley: University of California Press, 2014), 34-35.

21 Ibid.

22 Kelly Lytle Hernandez, *City of Inmates: Conquest, Rebellion, and the Rise of Human Caging in Los Angeles* (Chapel Hill: The University of North Carolina Press, 2017), 139.

23 California Senate, *Apology Act for the 1930s Mexican Repatriation Program*, SB 670, 2005.

24 Hernandez, *City of Inmates*, 1-8.

25 Molina, *How Race is Made*, 120.

26 Ibid.

27 Florence Adams, *Latinos and Local Representation: Changing Realities, Emerging Theories* (New York: Garland Publishing, 2000), 12.

28 Elizabeth Mandeel, "The Bracero Program 1942-64," *American International Journal of Contemporary Research*, Vol. 4, No. 1 (January 2014): 172.

29 Molina, *How Race is Made*, 134.

30 "The Japanese American Evacuation and Resettlement: A Digital Archive," *University of California Berkley*, accessed January 14, 2020, http://bancroft.berkeley.edu/collections/jais/timeline_event_feb42. html.

31 Michael Wines, "The Long History of the US Government Asking Americans Whether They Are Citizens," *NYT*, July 12, 2019, https://www.nytimes.com/2019/07/12/us/the-long-history-of-the-us-

government-asking-americans-whether-they-are-citizens.html.

32 *Korematsu v. US*, 323 US 214, 219-220 (1944).

33 *Plyler v. Doe*, 457 US 202, 225 (1982).

34 Brad Plummer, "Congress tried to fix immigration back in 1986. Why did it fail?" *The Washington Post*, January 30, 2013, https://www. washingtonpost.com/news/wonk/wp/2013/01/30/in-1986-congress-tried-to-solve-immigration-why-didnt-it-work/; "A Reagan Legacy: Amnesty for Illegal Immigrants," *NPR*, July 4, 2010, https://www.npr. org/templates/story/story.php?storyId=128303672.

35 *Matter of S-K-*, 23 I&N Dec. 936, 958 (BIA 2006).

Chapter 3

1 John Burnett, "Undocumented Irish Caught in Trump's Immigration Dragnet," NPR, January 22, 2018, https://www.npr. org/2018/01/22/578930256/undocumented-irish-unexpectedly-caught-in-trumps-immigration-dragnet.

2 Fintan O'Toole, "We are undocumented but they are illegal," *The Irish Times*, March 7, 2017, https://www.irishtimes.com/opinion/fintan-o-toole-we-are-undocumented-but-they-are-illegal-1.2999846.

3 Simon Carswell, "Ted Cruz vows to deport Irish immigrant 'Tommy O'Malley,'" *The Irish Times*, February 23, 2016.

4 Burnett, "Undocumented Irish Caught."

5 Kenan Malik, *The Meaning of Race: Race, History and Culture in Western Society* (New York, New York University Press, 1996).

6 Kenan Malik, *Strange Fruit: Why Both Sides are Wrong in the Race Debate* (Oxford, Oneworld Publications, 2008).

7 See Malik, Chapter One in *Strange Fruit*.

8 Ibid., 13.

9 See Malik, Chapter Two in *The Meaning of Race*.

10 Ibid.

11 Malik, *Strange Fruit*, 35.

12 "The History of the Word 'Xenophobia': The word isn't as old as you might think," The Merriam-Webster Dictionary, accessed January 7, 2020, https://www.merriam-webster.com/words-at-play/a-short-

history-of-xenophobia.

13 Lixing Sun, "Xenophobia in the Light of Evolution: On the Origins of Anti-Immigration Sentiment," *The Evolution Institute*, February 1, 2017, https://evolution-institute.org/xenophobia-in-the-light-of-evolution-on-the-origins-of-anti-immigration-sentiment/.

14 Ibid.

15 The origins of xenophobia," *The New Scientist*, issue 3068, April 9, 2016.

16 Sun, "Xenophobia in Light of Evolution."

17 Ibid.

18 Molina, *How Race is Made*, 39.

19 Ibid.

20 Ibid.

21 Ibid., 40.

22 Ibid., 42.

23 See generally, Molina, *How Race is Made*, 147.

24 Fitzgerald, *Culling the Masses*, 137.

25 Ibid., 138.

26 Ibid., 102, 107.

27 Caleb Melby, et al., "Trump's Immigration Ban Excludes Countries with Business Ties," *Bloomberg*, June 26, 2018, https://www.bloomberg.com/graphics/2017-trump-second-immigration-ban-conflict-of-interest/.

28 Fitzgerald, *Culling the Masses*, 137.

29 Ibid., 91.

30 Ibid., 138.

31 Senator John Box, "Immigration Restriction," *Congressional Record*, 69, no. 3 (1928).

32 Fitzgerald, *Culling the Masses*, 138.

33 "Mass Incarceration Fact Sheet for America's Concentration Camps: Remembering The Japanese American Experience," *Japanese American National Museum*, accessed January 7, 2020, http://www.janm.org/nrc/resources/accmass/.

34 US Congress, House of Rep., Select Committee Investigating National

Defense Migration, *San Francisco Hearings*, 77th Congress, 2nd Session, 1942.

35 "The Untold Story: Japanese-Americans' WWII Internment in Hawaii," *NBC*, August 2, 2014, https://www.nbcnews.com/news/asian-america/untold-story-japanese-americans-wwii-internment-hawaii-n170746.

36 O'Toole, "We are undocumented."

37 Fitzgerald, *Culling the Masses*, 333.

38 Ibid., 139.

39 Ibid., 334.

40 Ibid., 341.

41 Molina, *How Race is Made*, 133.

42 Ibid., 130.

43 Ibid., 134.

Chapter 4

1 Karl Marx, "Chapter XIX" in *Theories of Surplus Value Vol. 3* (Moscow: Progress Publishers ,1969).

2 Ibid.

3 Karl Marx, "The General Law of Capitalist Accumulation," in *Critique of Political Economy Volume No. 1*, trans. by Ben Fowkes (Hardmondsworth: Penguin Books, 1976).

4 Jeffrey S. Passel and D'Vera Cohn, "Occupations of unauthorized immigrant workers," *Pew Research Center*, November 3, 2016, 1, https://www.pewresearch.org/hispanic/2016/11/03/occupations-of-unauthorized-immigrant-workers/.

5 Eric A. Ruark, "Illegal Immigration & Agribusiness: The Effect on the Agriculture Industry of Converting to a Legal Workforce," *FAIR*, April 2013, https://www.fairus.org/sites/default/files/2017-08/agribusiness_rev2013.pdf, 1.

6 Ibid.

7 Ibid., 18.

8 Ibid., 16-17.

9 Eduardo Porter, "Short of Workers, US Builders and Farmers Crave

More Immigrants," *The New York Times*, April 3, 2019, https://www.nytimes.com/2019/04/03/business/economy/immigration-labor-economy.html.

10 Stephen G. Bronars, "A Vanishing Breed: How the Decline in US Farm Laborers Over the Last Decade Has Hurt the US Economy and Slowed Production on American Farms," *PNAE*, July 2015, 1, https://research.newamericaneconomy.org/wp-content/uploads/2015/08/PNAE_FarmLabor_August-3-3.pdf.

11 Stephen G. Bronars, "No Longer Home Grown: How Labor Shortages are Increasing America's Reliance on Imported Fresh Produce and Slowing US Economic Growth," *PNAE*, March 2014, 20, http://research.newamericaneconomy.org/wp-content/uploads/2014/03/no-longer-home-grown.pdf.

12 Preston Huennekens, "Unlimited Cheap Farm Labor: Evaluating H-2A Disclosure Data," *Center for Immigration Studies*, August 6, 2018, https://cis.org/Report/Unlimited-Cheap-Farm-Labor-Evaluating-H2A-Disclosure-Data.

13 Stuart Anderson, "What the Latest Border Statistics Really Mean," *Forbes*, March 7, 2019; Robert Warren, "Sharp Multiyear Decline in Undocumented Immigration Suggests Progress at US-Mexico Border, Not a National Emergency," *Center for Migration Studies*, February 27, 2019, doi: 10.14240/cmsesy022719.

14 Jason Richwine, "There Is No 'Labor Shortage,'" *Center for Immigration Studies*, April 16, 2019, https://cis.org/Report/There-No-Labor-Shortage.

15 Paul Harris, "Undocumented workers' grim reality: speak out on abuse and risk deportation," *The Guardian*, March 18, 2013, https://www.theguardian.com/world/2013/mar/28/undocumented-migrants-worker-abuse-deportation.

16 "Office of Foreign Labor Certification Annual Report," *US Department of Labor*, 2016, 15, https://www.foreignlaborcert.doleta.gov/pdf/OFLC_Annual_Report_FY2016.pdf.

17 Ruth Umoh, "The US has a shortage of tech workers. Here's how kids and schools can solve the problem," *CNBC*, August 23, 2017,

https://www.cnbc.com/2017/08/23/why-we-have-a-shortage-of-tech-workers-in-the-u-s.html.

18 Daniel Costa, "Stem labor shortages?: Microsoft report distorts reality about computing occupations," *Economic Policy Institute*, November 19, 2012.

19 Data compiled from government Labor Condition Application filings—*Immihelp*, last accessed, January 3, 2020, https://www.immihelp.com/employer/MICROSOFT+CORP/2593482/applications.

20 Costa, "Stem labor shortages?"

21 Ibid.

22 US Congress, Senate, The Subcommittee on Immigration and the National Interest, *The Impact of High-Skilled Immigration on US Workers*, February 25, 2016, 2, https://www.judiciary.senate.gov/imo/media/doc/02-25-16%20Hira%20Testimony.pdf.

23 Ibid.

24 Ibid., 3.

25 Ibid.

26 Ibid.

27 Ibid.

28 Ibid., 10.

29 Ibid.

30 Anthony Gabb, "The Uber Crash Is Just the Start: How the Gig Economy Threatens the Future of Work," *Truthout*, March 26, 2018, https://truthout.org/articles/the-uber-crash-is-just-the-start-how-the-gig-economy-threatens-the-future-of-work/.

31 Ibid.

32 Ibid.

33 "The Productivity-Pay Gap," *Economic Policy Institute*, Updated July 2019, https://www.epi.org/productivity-pay-gap/.

34 Gabb, "Gig Economy."

Chapter 5

1 Congressional Research Service, Recent Migration to the United States from Central America: Frequently Asked Questions, by Jill H.

Wilson et. al, R45489, Washington D.C.: CRS, 2019, https://fas.org/sgp/crs/row/R45489.pdf, 5-6.

2   Ibid.

3   Vladimir Lenin, "Export of Capital," in *Imperialism, the Highest Stage of Capitalism*, (Moscow: Progress Publishers, 1963).

4   Lenin, "Concentration of Production and Monopolies," and "Export of Capital," in *Imperialism*.

5   Lenin, "Division of the World among the Great Powers," in *Imperialism*.

6   Greg Grandin, *Empire's Workshop: Latin America, the United States, and the Rise of the New Imperialism*, (New York: Owl Books, 2007).

7   Grandin, *Empire's*, 17.

8   Ibid.

9   Ibid., 20.

10 Ibid., 2.

11 Ibid., 22.

12 Ibid., 22-3.

13 Ibid., 23-4.

14 Ibid., 27.

15 Ibid., 35, 39.

16 Ibid., 48-50.

17 Ibid., 50.

18 Ibid., 71.

19 Ibid., 187.

20 Ibid., 187-8.

21 Ibid., 198; CEPAL, "Poverty Increased in 2016 in Latin America and Reached 30.7% of the Population, a Percentage Seen Holding Steady in 2017," *CEPAL*, (December 2017). https://www.cepal.org/en/pressreleases/poverty-increased-2016-latin-america-and-reached-307-population-percentage-seen.

22 Grandin, *Empire's*, 200.

23 Ibid., 202-5.

24 InSight Crime and the Center for Latin American & Latino Studies, *MS 13 in the Americas: How the World's Most Notorious Gang Defies Logic, Resists Destruction*, by Steven Dudley et. al, (2019), 14-15, https://

www.insightcrime.org/wp-content/uploads/2018/02/MS13-in-the-Americas-InSight-Crime-English.pdf.

25 Ibid., 15.

26 Ibid.; James Cohen, "Capitalist Transformation, social violence and transnational migration," *Revue de recherche en civilisation américaine*, 7 (December 2017): 6, http://journals.openedition.org/rrca/853.

27 Cohen, "Capitalist Transformation," 7 (discussing Dawn Paley, *Drug War Capitalism*, (AK Press 2014).

28 Kanta Kumari Rigaud, et. al, *Groundswell: Preparing for Internal Climate Migration*, (Washington D.C.: The World Bank 2018), 110.

29 Ibid.

30 Ibid., xxii.

31 Grandin, "Bringing It All Back Home: The Politics of New Imperialism," in *Empire's*.

32 Ibid.

33 Ibid., 120.

34 Ibid., 122-3.

35 Ibid., 139.

36 Ibid., 137-9.

37 Ibid., 131-4.

38 Ibid., 134.

39 Ibid., 228; see generally, Edward Herman, Noam Chomsky, *Manufacturing Consent: the Political Economy of the Mass Media*, (New York: Pantheon Books, 2002).

40 Grandin, *Empire's*, 130.

41 Naomi Klein, "Capitalism vs. the Climate," *The Nation*, (November 9, 2011), https://www.thenation.com/article/capitalism-vs-climate/.

42 Danny Sjursen, "The Disturbing Parallels Between US policing at Home and Military Tactics Abroad," *The Nation*, (October 12, 2017), https://www.thenation.com/article/archive/the-disturbing-parallels-between-us-policing-at-home-and-military-tactics-abroad/.

43 Ibid.

44 Ibid.

45 Ibid.

Chapter 6

1   The story and data in this paragraph come from Eyder Peralta, "You Say You're An American, But What If You Had to Prove it Or Be Deported?" *NPR*, December 22, 2016, https://www.npr.org/sections/thetwo-way/2016/12/22/504031635/you-say-you-re-an-american-but-what-if-you-had-to-prove-it-or-be-deported.

2   8 U.S.C. 1101(a).

3   Rosa Luxemburg, "The Nation-State and The Proletariat," in *The National Question*, Rosa Luxemburg Archive, 2008).

4   Ibid.

5   Ibid.

6   Ibid.

7   Ibid.

8   Malik, *Race*, 134.

9   Ibid.

10 Karl Marx & Friedrich Engels, "Civil Society and the Conception of History," in *The German Ideology* (Moscow: Progress Publishers, 1968).

11 Malik, *Race*, 58.

12 Michael Parenti, *Democracy for the Few*, 7th ed. (Boston: Bedford/St. Martin's, 2002), 42-52.

13 Ibid., 43.

14 Ibid., 49-53.

15 Louis Althusser, *Ideology and Ideological State Apparatuses*, from *Lenin and Philosophy and other Essays* (New York: Monthly Review Press, 1971).

16 Ibid.

17 Malik, *Race*, 136.

18 Neil Larry Shumsky, *Noah Webster and the Invention of Immigration, The New England Quarterly*, 81, No.1 (Mar., 2008), 130.

19 Malik, *Race*, 136.

20 Ibid.,136-40.

21 Ibid.

Chapter 7

1   Nicole Chaves, "Border Patrol Agent acquitted in fatal shooting of Mexican teen," *CNN*, last updated November 22, 2018, https://www.cnn.com/2018/11/22/us/border-patrol-agent-acquitted-mexican-teen-killing/index.html.

2   Rafael Carranza and Rob O'Dell, "Border Patrol agent Lonnie Swartz found not guilty in cross-border slaying of Mexican teen," *The Arizona Republic*, last updated May 11, 2018, https://www.azcentral.com/story/news/politics/border-issues/2018/04/23/border-patrol-agent-lonnie-swartz-found-not-guilty-cross-border-slaying-mexican-teen/544197002/.

3   In its 100-year history, no Border Patrol agent has ever been killed by a rock. In records dating back as far as 1792, there is only one known police officer who was killed by a rock in US history. See "Border Patrol Office Who Shot Unarmed Teenager on Mexican Soil Is Acquitted of Manslaughter Charges," *Democracy Now!* November 27, 2018, https://www.democracynow.org/2018/11/27/border_patrol_officer_who_shot_unarmed.

4   Ibid.

5   Chaves, "Agent acquitted in fatal shooting."

6   Nick Vaughan-Williams, *Border Politics*, (Edinburgh: Edinburgh University Press 2009), 1.

7   Ibid., 3.

8   Ibid., 132.

9   Greg Grandin, *The End of the Myth: From the Frontier to the Border Wall in the Mind of America*, (New York: Metropolitan Books 2019), 273-75.

10 Ibid., 29, 82.

11 Ibid., 67.

12 Ibid., 199.

13 Ibid., 82.

14 Ibid., 199.

15 Ibid., 199-200.

16 Ibid., 199, 253-4.

17 Victor Reklaitis, "Here are the companies poised to profit from the

Trump border wall," *Marketwatch*, February 25, 2019, https://www.marketwatch.com/story/here-are-the-companies-poised-to-profit-from-the-trump-border-wall-2019-02-22.

18 David Kyle, Zai Liang, "Migration Merchants: Human Smuggling from Ecuador and China," *The Center for Comparative Immigration Studies*, Working Paper 43 (October 2001): 3, https://ccis.ucsd.edu/_files/wp43.pdf.

19 Grandin, *The End of the Myth*, 166; Greg Grandin, "Border Patrol Has Been a Cult of Brutality Since 1924," *The Intercept*, January 12, 2019, https://theintercept.com/2019/01/07/cbp-border-patrol-enforcement-law-course/.

20 Grandin, *The End of the Myth*, 250-1.

21 Ibid.

22 Ibid., 259.

23 "Debate at the Stuttgart Congress [1907] on immigration," trans. by Ed Potts, *Medium*, September 13, 2018, https://medium.com/@simonhannah/debate-at-the-stuttgart-congress-1907-on-immigration-9971f565da90.

24 Grandin, "Cult of Brutality."

25 Stuart Anderson, "How Many More Deaths? The Moral Case for a Temporary Worker Program," *National Foundation for American Policy* (March 2013): 3, http://www.nfap.com/pdf/NFAP%20Policy%20Brief%20Moral%20Case%20For%20a%20Temporary%20Worker%20Program%20March%202013.pdf.

26 Anderson, "How many More Deaths?", 1.

27 Stuart Anderson, "What the Latest Border Statistics Really Mean," *Forbes*, March 7, 2019.

28 Ibid.

29 Ibid.

30 *Hernandez v. Mesa*, 589 US ____, slip op. No. 17-1678, (2020).

31 Giorgio Agamben, *Homo Sacer*, (Stanford: Stanford University Press, 1998), 9; Vaughan-Williams, *Border Politics*, 132-3; 138.

32 "The Constitution in the 100-Mile Border Zone," *ACLU*, accessed September 21, 2019,https://www.aclu.org/other/constitution-100-

mile-border-zone?redirect=national-security_technology-and-liberty/
are-you-living-constitution-free-zone.

33　Grandin, "Cult of Brutality."

34　ACLU, "Constitution in the 100-Mile Border Zone."

35　Agamben, *Sacer*, 6-9.

36　Thomas Carl Wall, "Au Hasard," in *Politics, Metaphysics, and Death, Essays on Giorgio Agamben's Homo Sacer*, ed. Andrew Norris, (Durham: Duke University Press, 2005).

37　Agamben, *Sacer*, 6-17.

38　Ibid., 15-17.

39　Ibid., 142.

40　See Ibid., 27.

41　Vaughan-Williams, *Border Politics*, 6.

42　Ibid., 19-22.

43　Michael D. Shear and Maggie Haberman, "Mexico Agreed to Take Border Actions Months Before Trump Announced Tariff Deal," *NY Times*, June 8, 2019, https://www.nytimes.com/2019/06/08/us/politics/trump-mexico-deal-tariffs.html.

44　Vaughan-Williams, *Border Politics*, 39.

45　ACLU, "Constitution in the 100-Mile Border Zone."

46　Ibid.

47　Ibid.

48　Grandin, "Cult of Brutality."

49　Grandin, *The End of the Myth*, 129-30.

50　Ibid., 131.

51　Ibid., 190-1.

52　Ibid., 228-9.

53　Ibid., 226.

54　Ibid., 248.

Chapter 8

1　Katie McDonough, "Scenes from a Sanctuary City," *Splinter*, January 12, 2018, https://splinternews.com/scenes-from-a-sanctuary-city-1822025508.

2   Katie McDonough, "The Endless Limbo of Life Between ICE Check-Ins," *Splinter*, April 3, 2017, https://splinternews.com/the-endless-limbo-of-life-between-ice-check-ins-1794266500.

3   McDonough, "Scenes from a Sanctuary City."

4   Ibid.

5   Ibid.

6   Katie McDonough, "A Short, Brutal History of ICE," *Splinter*, February 2, 2018, https://splinternews.com/a-short-brutal-history-of-ice-1822641556.

7   Ibid.

8   Samantha Hauptman, *The Criminalization of Immigration: The Post 9/11 Moral Panic* (El Paso: LFB Scholarly Publishing LLC, 2013), 3.

9   Ibid., 6.

10   Ibid.

11   McDonough, "A Short, Brutal History of ICE."

12   Pinto, "Ice is Targeting Political Opponents."

13   Kim Zetter, "Police Contract with Spy Tool Maker Prohibits Talking About Device's Use," *Wired*, March 4, 2014, https://www.wired.com/2014/03/harris-stingray-nda/.

14   US Congress, House, Committee on Oversight and Government Reform, *Law Enforcement Use of Cell-Site Simulation Technologies: Privacy Concerns and Recommendations*, 114th Congress, 2016, 5, https://www.hsdl.org/?view&did=797902.

15   Ibid.

16   Benjamin Fleury-Steiner, "Deportation Platforms: The AWS-ICE Alliance and the Fallacy of Explicit Agendas," *Surveillance & Society* 17(1/2) (2019): 107.

17   Rosalie Chan, "Read the internal letter sent by a group of Amazon employees asking the company to take a stand against ICE," *Business Insider*, July 11, 2019, https://www.businessinsider.com/amazon-employees-letter-protest-palantir-ice-camps-2019-7.

18   "Who's Behind ICE?" *Mijente* et. al, 3, accessed December 27, 2019, https://mijente.net/wp-content/uploads/2018/10/WHO%E2%80%99S-BEHIND-ICE_-The-Tech-and-Data-Companies-Fueling-

Deportations_v3-.pdf.

19 Ibid.

20 "Stingray Tracking Devices: Who's Got Them?" ACLU, last modified November 2018, https://www.aclu.org/issues/privacy-technology/surveillance-technologies/stingray-tracking-devices-whos-got-them.

21 Zetter, "Police Contract with Spy Tool Maker."

22 US Immigration and Customs Enforcement, "DHS Assistant Secretary Discusses Progress in War on Terror at Duke Law Symposium," News Release, (February 4, 2005), 6, https://www.ice.gov/doclib/news/library/speeches/garcia020405.pdf.

23 Human Rights Watch and Columbia Law School, *Illusion of Justice: Human Rights Abuses in US Terrorism Prosecutions* (US: Human Rights Watch, 2014), 21, https://www.hrw.org/sites/default/files/reports/usterrorism0714_ForUpload_0_0_0.pdf.

24 Ibid., 22.

25 Masha Gessen, *The Brothers: The Road to an American Tragedy* (New York: Riverhead Books, 2015), 135, 234, 243.

26 Louise Richardson, *What Terrorists Want: Understanding the Enemy, Containing the Threat*, (New York: Random House, 2006), 56.

27 Ibid., 57.

28 Ibid.

29 Gessen, *The Brothers*, 170.

30 "Profiling Who ICE Detains - Few Committed Any Crime," *TRAC*, October 9, 2018, https://trac.syr.edu/immigration/reports/530/.

31 Uri Freedman, "How Many Attacks Will it Take Until the White-Supremacist Threat is Taken Seriously?" *The Atlantic*, August 4, 2019, https://www.theatlantic.com/politics/archive/2019/08/how-can-fbi-fight-far-right-extremism-ideology/595435/.

32 Nick Pinto, "ICE is Targeting Political Opponents for Deportation, Ravi Ragbir and Rights Groups Say in Court," *The Intercept*, February 9, 2018, https://theintercept.com/2018/02/09/ravi-ragbir-ice-immigration-deportation/.

33 *Ragbir v. Sessions*, 18-cv-236 (KBF) at 7 (S.D.N.Y. 2018).

34 Robert J. Art and Louise Richardson, *Democracy and Counterterrorism:*

Lessons from the Past, (Washington D.C.: US Institute of Peace, 2007), 1.

Chapter 9

1   The story in this paragraph comes from Judith A. Greene, et al., *Indefensible: A Decade of Mass Incarceration of Migrants Prosecuted for Crossing the Border* (Grassroots Leadership and Justice Strategies, 2016), 128-130, http://grassrootsleadership.org/sites/default/files/reports/indefensible_book_web.pdf.

2   Ibid., 7.

3   Bryan Schatz, "A Day in the 'Assembly-Line' Court That Prosecutes 70 Border Crossers in 2 Hours," *Mother Jones*, July 21, 2017, https://www.motherjones.com/politics/2017/07/a-day-in-the-assembly-line-court-that-sentences-46-border-crossers-in-2-hours/.

4   Greene, *Indefensible*, 31.

5   Ibid., 78.

6   Ibid., 36.

7   Ibid., 38.

8   Ibid., 58.

9   Ibid., 39-40.

10   Ibid., 129.

11   Jeremy Slack et al., "In the Shadow of the Wall: Family Separation, Immigration Enforcement and Security," *The Center for Latin American Studies, University of Arizona*, (March 2013): 15, https://papers.ssrn.com/sol3/papers.cfm?abstract_id=2633204.

12   Greene, *Indefensible*, 26-7.

13   "Immigration Now 52 Percent of All Federal Criminal Prosecutions," *TRAC*, November 28, 2016, https://trac.syr.edu/tracreports/crim/446/.

14   Ibid.

15   Ibid.

16   Greene, *Indefensible*, viii

17   Greene, *Indefensible*, 8.

18   "FAQs: Global Poverty Line Update," *The World Bank*, September 30, 2015, https://www.worldbank.org/en/topic/poverty/brief/global-poverty-line-faq.

19 Arjun Sethi, Holly Kirby, "Incarceration Across State Lines," *Al Jazeera America*, February 12, 2014, http://america.aljazeera.com/opinions/2014/2/prison-overcrowdingaboonforprivateprisons.html.

20 Shane Bauer, "The Corrections Corporation of America, by the Numbers," *Mother Jones*, July/August 2016, https://www.motherjones.com/politics/2016/06/cca-corrections-corperation-america-private-prisons-company-profile/.

21 Michael Cohen, "How for-profit prisons have become the biggest lobby no one is talking about," *The Washington Post*, April 28, 2015, (citing CCA's own 2014 report), https://www.washingtonpost.com/posteverything/wp/2015/04/28/how-for-profit-prisons-have-become-the-biggest-lobby-no-one-is-talking-about/.

22 "The 287(g) Program: An Overview," *American Immigration Council*, August 23, 2019, https://www.americanimmigrationcouncil.org/research/287g-program-immigration.

23 Renee Feltz, Stokely Baksh, "Business of Detention," in *Beyond Walls and Cages: Prisons, Borders, and Global Crises*, ed. Jenna M. Lloyd, et al., (Athens: The University of Georgia Press, 2012), 125.

24 *Jennings v. Rodriguez*, No. 15-204, slip op. (US February 27, 2018) (Breyer, J., dissenting).

25 Ibid.

26 "Immigration and Nationality Act—Mandatory and Prolonged Detention—Access to Bond Hearings—Jennings v. Rodriguez," *Harvard Law Review*, Vol. 132 (November 2018): 423.

27 Cesar Cuauhtemoc Garcia Hernandez, "Immigration Detention as Punishment," *UCLA Law Review*, 61 (2014): 1351.

28 Ibid., 1352-3.

29 David Grable, "Personhood Under the Due Process Clause: A Constitutional Analysis of the Illegal Immigration Reform and Immigrant Responsibility Act of 1996," *Cornell Law Review* 83, (1998): 839.

30 Agamben, *Sacer*, 174.

31 Judith Butler, *Precarious Life: The Powers of Mourning and Violence* (New York: Verso, 2006), 58-9.

32   *Harvard Law Review*, "Mandatory and Prolonged Detention," 417.

33   Anne Bonds, "Building Prisons, Building Poverty," in *Beyond Walls*.

34   Ruth Wilson Gilmore, *Golden Gulag: Prisons, Surplus, Crisis, and Opposition in Globalizing California* (Berkley: University of California Press, 2007), 26-7.

35   Bonds, *Beyond Walls*, 116.

36   Holly Kirby, "Locked Up & Shipped Away: Interstate Prisoner Transfers and the Private Prison Industry," *Grassroots Leadership*, (November 2013), http://grassrootsleadership.org/sites/default/files/uploads/locked_up_shipped_away.pdf.

37   Sethi, "Incarceration Across State Lines."

38   Greene, *Indefensible*, 108-9.

39   Miriam Jordan, "An Arizona Teacher Helped Migrants. Jurors Couldn't Decide if It Was a Crime," *New York Times*, June 11, 2019, https://www.nytimes.com/2019/06/11/us/scott-warren-arizona-deaths.html.

40   Ibid.

41   Alex Devoid, "Federal prosecutors to retry case of border-aid worker Scott Warren," *Arizona Daily Star*, July 2, 2019, https://tucson.com/news/local/federal-prosecutors-to-retry-case-of-border-aid-worker-scott/article_64a9161e-9ce5-11e9-9848-3346d62a5d69.html.

42   Ron Medvescek, "Border aid volunteers sentenced to probation in Tucson," *Arizona Daily Star*, March 1, 2019, https://tucson.com/news/local/border-aid-volunteers-sentenced-to-probation-in-tucson/article_1160a3c2-3c74-11e9-bd57-873b4471925b.html.

43   Jeffrey Sessions, "Memorandum for All Federal Prosecutors: Renewed Commitment to Criminal Immigration Enforcement," *Office of the Attorney General*, April 11, 2017, https://www.justice.gov/opa/press-release/file/956841/download.

44   Lorne Matalon, "Extending 'Zero Tolerance' to People Who Help Migrants Along the Border," *NPR*, May 28, 2019, https://www.npr.org/2019/05/28/725716169/extending-zero-tolerance-to-people-who-help-migrants-along-the-border.

45   Kristine Phillips, "They left food and water for migrants in the desert. Now they might go to prison," *The Washington Post*, January 20, 2019,

https://www.washingtonpost.com/nation/2019/01/20/they-left-food-water-migrants-desert-now-they-might-go-prison/.

46   Charles D. Weisselberg, "The Exclusion and Detention of Aliens: Lessons from the Lives of Ellen Knauff and Ignatz Mezei," *University of Pennsylvania Law Review* 143, (April 1995): 1034.

Chapter 10

1   The circumstances surrounding this case can be found in Bea Bischoff, "Jeff Sessions is Hijacking Immigration Law," June 13, 2018, https:// slate.com/news-and-politics/2018/06/in-matter-of-a-b-jeff-sessions-hijacked-immigration-law-by-abusing-a-rarely-used-provision.html.

2   8 USC. section 1101(a)(42)(A).

3   8 USC. section 1158(a)(2).

4   *Matter of A-B-*, 27 I&N Dec. 316 (AG 2018).

5   *Matter of S-E-G-*, 24 I&N Dec. 579 (BIA 2008); *Matter of E-A-G-*, 24 I&N Dec. 591 (BIA 2008).

6   *Matter M-E-V-G-*, 26 I&N Dec. 227, 250 (BIA 2014).

7   Banks Miller, et. al, *Immigration Judges and US Asylum Policy* (Philadelphia: University of Pennsylvania Press, 2015), 5.

8   Ibid., 17, 49.

9   Ibid., 49.

10   Ibid., 17.

11   Susan Gzesh, "Central Americans and Asylum Policy in the Reagan Era," *Migration Policy Institute*, April 1, 2006, https://www.migrationpolicy.org/article/central-americans-and-asylum-policy-reagan-era.

12   Ibid.

13   Ibid.

14   "Asylum Representation Rates Have Fallen Amid Rising Denial Rates," *TRAC*, November 28, 2017, https://trac.syr.edu/immigration/reports/491/.

15   Miller, *Immigration Judges*, 70.

16   Ibid., 1.

17   "Asylum Outcome Continues to Depend on the Judge Assigned,"

TRAC, November 20, 2017, https://trac.syr.edu/immigration/reports/490/.

18 Ibid.

19 Ibid.

20 Miller, *Immigration Judges*, 1.

21 Ibid., 22.

22 Ibid., 82.

23 Jennifer Ludden, "Immigration Crackdown Overwhelms Judges," *NPR*, February 9, 2009, https://www.npr.org/templates/story/story.php?storyId=100420476.

24 Karl Marx, "Preface to a Contribution to the Critique of Political Economy," in *The Marx Engels Reader*, ed. Robert Tucker, 2d ed. (New York: W.W. Norton & Company, 1978), 4.

25 Michael Mandel, "Marxism and the Rule of Law," *UNB Law Journal* 35 (1986): 20.

26 Ibid., 20-1.

27 Glenn Greenwald, *With Liberty and Justice for Some: How the Law is Used to Destroy Equality and Protect the Powerful* (New York: Metropolitan Books, 2011), 3.

28 Ibid., 9-10.

29 Mandel, "The Rule of Law," 24.

30 Ibid., 25.

31 Karl Marx, "Critique of the Gotha Program," in *Marx and Engels Selected Works, Volume Three*, (Moscow: Progress Publishers, 1970).

32 Agamben, *Sacer*, 15-17.

33 *Price v. United States*, 174 US 373, 375-6 (1899).

34 Greenwald, "The Origin of Elite Immunity," in *With Liberty and Justice*.

Chapter 11

1 Jane's story in this paragraph is taken from Logan Hullinger, "Lancaster woman sues federal government over immigrant status," *York Dispatch*, August 27, 2019, https://www.yorkdispatch.com/story/news/politics/2019/08/27/caught-up-broken-u-visa-process-lancaster-immigrant-sues-federal-government/2071028001/.

2   "Number of Form I-918, Petition for U Nonimmigrant Status by Fiscal Year, Quarter, and Case Status Fiscal Years 2009-2019," *USCIS*, last accessed March 24, 2020.

3   Isabela Dias, "She Helped Convict Her Rapist. ICE Deported Her Anyway," *The Nation*, April 1, 2019, https://www.thenation.com/article/archive/u-visa-immigration-ice-uscis/.

4   Ibid.

5   "Visa Bulletin for December 2019, Number 36 Volume X," *US Department of State*, November 8, 2019, https://travel.state.gov/content/dam/visas/Bulletins/visabulletin_december2019.pdf.

6   "Historical National Average Process Time (in Months) for All USCIS Offices for Select Forms by Fiscal Year," *US Citizenship and Immigration Services*, last accessed March 23, 2020, https://egov.uscis.gov/processing-times/historic-pt.

7   Meagan Flynn, "Citizenship service conspired with ICE to 'trap' immigrants at visa interviews, ACLU says," *Washington Post*, August 15, 2018, https://www.washingtonpost.com/news/morning-mix/wp/2018/08/15/citizenship-service-conspired-with-ice-to-trap-immigrants-at-green-card-interviews-aclu-says/.

8   "Unlawful Presence and Bars to Admissibility," *USCIS*, last modified May 6, 2019, https://www.uscis.gov/legal-resources/unlawful-presence-and-bars-admissibility.

9   Agamben, "Chapter One," in *Homo Sacer*.

10 "Application for Naturalization Form N-400," *US Citizenship and Immigration Services*, September 17, 2019 ed, 14, https://www.uscis.gov/system/files_force/files/form/n-400.pdf.

11 Allyson Escobar, "Most of us would fail the US citizenship test, survey finds," *NBC*, October 12, 2018, https://www.nbcnews.com/news/latino/most-us-would-fail-u-s-citizenship-test-survey-finds-n918961.

12 Katherine Tonkiss, "What's So Bad about Citizenship Testing?" *E-International Relations*, November 28, 2014, https://www.e-ir.info/2014/11/28/whats-so-bad-about-citizenship-testing/.

13 David Scott Fitzgerald, "The History of Racialized Citizenship," in *The Oxford Handbook of Citizenship*, ed. Ayelet Shachar, et. al, (Oxford:

Oxford University Press, 2017), 138.

14   Laura Bingham, et. al, *Unmaking Americans: Insecure Citizenship in the United States* (Open Society Foundations, 2019), 62-63, https://www.justiceinitiative.org/uploads/e05c542e-0db4-40cc-a3ed-2d73abcfd37f/unmaking-americans-insecure-citizenship-in-the-united-states-report-20190916.pdf.

15   Ibid., 50.

16   Ibid., 52-5.

17   Ibid., 58.

18   Ibid., 13.

19   Masha Gessen, "In America, Naturalized Citizens No Longer Have an Assumption of Permanence," *The New Yorker*, June 18, 2018, https://www.newyorker.com/news/our-columnists/in-america-naturalized-citizens-no-longer-have-an-assumption-of-permanence.

20   *FTC v. Ruberoid Co.*, 343 US 470, 487 (1952).

21   *Chevron v Natural Res. Def. Council, Inc.*, 467 US 837 (1984); Jill E. Family, "Immigration Law Allies and Administrative Law Adversaries," *Georgetown Immigration Law Journal* 32 (December 2017): 104.

22   David Bier, "Immigration Application Denial Rates Jump 37% Under Trump," *Cato*, November 15, 2018, https://www.cato.org/blog/immigration-application-denials-jump-37-percent-under-trump.

23   Sabeel Rahman, "Reconstructing the Administrative State in an Era of Economic and Democratic Crisis," *Harvard Law Review* 131 (April 2018): 1682-3.

24   Ibid., 1685.

25   Ibid.

26   Ibid., 1688.

27   Ibid., 1690.

28   Ibid., 1695.

29   Ibid., 1711.

Chapter 12

1   Ben Gitis and Laura Collins, "The Budgetary and Economic Costs of Addressing Unauthorized Immigration: Alternative

Strategies," *American Action Forum*, March 6, 2015, https://www.americanactionforum.org/research/the-budgetary-and-economic-costs-of-addressing-unauthorized-immigration-alt/.

2   "Estimated Earnings and Tax Contributions of Undocumented Immigrants, 2016," *PNAE*, last accessed January 4, 2020, https://www.newamericaneconomy.org/issues/undocumented-immigrants/#economic-contributors,-not-criminals.

3   Lisa Christensen Gee, et. al, "Undocumented Immigrants' State & Local Tax Contributions," *Institute on Taxation & Economic Policy*, March 1, 2017, https://itep.org/undocumented-immigrants-state-local-tax-contributions-2017/.

4   Nina Roberts, "Undocumented immigrants quietly pay billions into Social Security and receive no benefits," *Marketplace*, January 28, 2019, https://www.marketplace.org/2019/01/28/undocumented-immigrants-quietly-pay-billions-social-security-and-receive-no/.

5   Angela Nagle, "The Left Case Against Open Borders," *American Affairs*, vol. II, Number 4, Winter 2018, https://americanaffairsjournal.org/2018/11/the-left-case-against-open-borders/, 17-30.

6   Karl Marx and Friedrich Engels, "Marx to Sigfrid Meyer and August Vogt in New York," in *Selected Correspondence* (Moscow: Progress Publishers, 1975), 220-4.

7   Ibid.

8   Fitzgerald, *Culling*, 345.

9   Ibid.

10 Ibid., 346.

11 Lee, "Open Borders."

12 Lori Robertson, "The DACA Population Numbers," *FactCheck*, January 12, 2018, https://www.factcheck.org/2018/01/daca-population-numbers/.

13 Serena Marshall, "Obama Has Deported More People Than Any Other President," *ABC News*, August 29, 2016, https://abcnews.go.com/Politics/obamas-deportation-policy-numbers/story?id=41715661.

14 Grandin, *Empire's Workshop*, 222.

15 See Hannah Arendt, "The 'Nation of Minorities' and the Stateless

People" in *The Origins of Totalitarianism*, (San Diego: Harvest Books, 1976).

16 Rosa Luxemburg, "The Right of Nations to Self-Determination," in *The National Question*, (Rosa Luxemburg Archive, 2008).

17 Ibid.

18 Kenan Malik, "Human rights mean nothing unless we defend real, threatened people," *The Guardian*, March 10, 2019, https://www.theguardian.com/commentisfree/2019/mar/10/human-rights-mean-nothing-unless-we-defend-real-threatened-people.

Chapter 13

1 See Agamben, *Homo Sacer*, 171.

2 See Arendt, *Totalitarianism*, 299-300.

3 Ibid., 298.

4 Ibid.

5 Rainer Forst, *Justice, Democracy, and the Right to Justification: Rainer Forst in Dialogue* (New York: Bloomsbury Academic, 2014), 7, 20.

6 Ibid., 201.

7 Rainer Forst, *The Right to Justification: Elements of a Constructivist Theory of Justice*, trans. Jeremy Flynn (New York: Columbia University Press 2014), 21.

8 Ibid., 205.

9 Ibid., 209-10, 214.

10 See Ibid., 217.

11 Forst, *In Dialogue*, 200-1.

12 Ibid., 201

13 Lee, "The Case for Open Borders."

14 Forst, *Right to Justification*, 222.

15 Karl Marx, "Estranged Labor" in *Economic & Philosophic Manuscripts of 1844*, trans. Martin Milligan (Moscow: Progress Publishers, 1959).

16 James Kwak, *Economism* (New York: Pantheon, 2017), 63.

17 Ibid., 86.

18 Ibid., 184, 186.

19 Forst, *Right to Justification*, 248.

20 Ibid.

21 Agamben, *Sacer*, 40.

22 Ibid.

23 Ibid., 140.

24 Forst, *Right to Justification*, 220.

25 Mandel, "Marxism and the Rule of Law," 33.

26 Karl Marx, *Capital: A Critique of Political Economy Volume No. 1*, trans. by Ben Fowkes (Hardmondsworth: Penguin Books, 1976), 416.

27 Tam Harbert, "Here's how much the 2008 bailouts really cost," MIT, February 21, 2019, https://mitsloan.mit.edu/ideas-made-to-matter/ heres-how-much-2008-bailouts-really-cost.

28 Ibid.

29 "An Economy for the 99%," *Oxfam*, January 2017, 2.

30 Ibid.

31 "US Muslims Concerned About Their Place in Society, but Continue to Believe in the American Dream," *Pew Research Center*, July 26, 2017, http://assets.pewresearch.org/wp-content/uploads/ sites/11/2017/07/25171611/US-MUSLIMS-FULL-REPORT.pdf.

32 Ibid.

33 Drew DeSilver, "US public seldom has welcomed refugees into country," *Pew Research Center*, November 19, 2015, https://www. pewresearch.org/fact-tank/2015/11/19/u-s-public-seldom-has- welcomed-refugees-into-country/.

34 See Maureen Baker and Mary-Anne Robeson, "Trade union reactions to women workers and their concerns," *The Canadian Journal of Sociology*, 6 no. 1 (1981): 19-31.

35 Forst, *Right to Justification*, 241.

36 David Deutsch, *The Beginning of Infinity: Explanations that Transform the World* (New York: Penguin Group, 2011), 64-5.

CULTURE, SOCIETY & POLITICS

The modern world is at an impasse. Disasters scroll across our smartphone screens and we're invited to like, follow or upvote, but critical thinking is harder and harder to find. Rather than connecting us in common struggle and debate, the internet has sped up and deepened a long-standing process of alienation and atomization. Zer0 Books wants to work against this trend. With critical theory as our jumping off point, we aim to publish books that make our readers uncomfortable. We want to move beyond received opinions.

Zer0 Books is on the left and wants to reinvent the left. We are sick of the injustice, the suffering and the stupidity that defines both our political and cultural world, and we aim to find a new foundation for a new struggle.

If this book has helped you to clarify an idea, solve a problem or extend your knowledge, you may want to check out our online content as well. Look for Zer0 Books: Advancing Conversations in the iTunes directory and for our Zer0 Books YouTube channel.

Popular videos include:

Žižek and the Double Blackmain
The Intellectual Dark Web is a Bad Sign
Can there be an Anti-SJW Left?
Answering Jordan Peterson on Marxism

Follow us on Facebook
at https://www.facebook.com/ZeroBooks and Twitter at https://
twitter.com/Zer0Books

Bestsellers from Zer0 Books include:

Give Them An Argument
Logic for the Left
Ben Burgis
Many serious leftists have learned to distrust talk of logic. This is
a serious mistake.
Paperback: 978-1-78904-210-8 ebook: 978-1-78904-211-5

Poor but Sexy
Culture Clashes in Europe East and West
Agata Pyzik
How the East stayed East and the West stayed West.
Paperback: 978-1-78099-394-2 ebook: 978-1-78099-395-9

An Anthropology of Nothing in Particular
Martin Demant Frederiksen
A journey into the social lives of meaninglessness.
Paperback: 978-1-78535-699-5 ebook: 978-1-78535-700-8

In the Dust of This Planet
Horror of Philosophy vol. 1
Eugene Thacker
In the first of a series of three books on the Horror of Philosophy,
In the Dust of This Planet offers the genre of horror as a way of
thinking about the unthinkable.
Paperback: 978-1-84694-676-9 ebook: 978-1-78099-010-1

Capitalist Realism
Is There No Alternative?
Mark Fisher
An analysis of the ways in which capitalism has presented itself
as the only realistic political-economic system.
Paperback: 978-1-84694-317-1 ebook: 978-1-78099-734-6

The End of Oulipo?

An Attempt to Exhaust a Movement
Lauren Elkin, Veronica Esposito
Paperback: 978-1-78099-655-4 ebook: 978-1-78099-656-1

Rebel Rebel

Chris O'Leary
David Bowie: every single song. Everything you want to know,
everything you didn't know.
Paperback: 978-1-78099-244-0 ebook: 978-1-78099-713-1

Kill All Normies

Angela Nagle
Online culture wars from 4chan and Tumblr to Trump.
Paperback: 978-1- 78535-543-1 ebook: 978-1-78535-544-8

Cartographies of the Absolute

Alberto Toscano, Jeff Kinkle
An aesthetics of the economy for the twenty-first century.
Paperback: 978-1-78099-275-4 ebook: 978-1-78279-973-3

Malign Velocities

Accelerationism and Capitalism
Benjamin Noys
Long listed for the Bread and Roses Prize 2015, *Malign Velocities*
argues against the need for speed, tracking acceleration
as the symptom of the ongoing crises of capitalism.
Paperback: 978-1-78279-300-7 ebook: 978-1-78279-299-4

Babbling Corpse

Vaporwave and the Commodification of Ghosts
Grafton Tanner
Paperback: 978-1-78279-759-3 ebook: 978-1-78279-760-9

Neglected or Misunderstood
The Radical Feminism of Shulamith Firestone
Victoria Margree
An interrogation of issues surrounding gender, biology,
sexuality, work and technology, and the ways in which our
imaginations continue to be in thrall to ideologies of maternity
and the nuclear family.
Paperback: 978-1-78535-539-4 ebook: 978-1-78535-540-0

How to Dismantle the NHS in 10 Easy Steps (Second Edition)
Youssef El-Gingihy
The story of how your NHS was sold off and why you will have
to buy private health insurance soon. A new expanded second
edition with chapters on junior doctors' strikes and government
blueprints for US-style healthcare.
Paperback: 978-1-78904-178-1 ebook: 978-1-78904-179-8

Digesting Recipes
The Art of Culinary Notation
Susannah Worth
A recipe is an instruction, the imperative tone of the expert, but
this constraint can offer its own kind of potential. A recipe need
not be a domestic trap but might instead offer escape – something
to fantasise about or aspire to.
Paperback: 978-1-78279-860-6 ebook: 978-1-78279-859-0

Most titles are published in paperback and as an ebook.
Paperbacks are available in traditional bookshops. Both print and
ebook formats are available online.
Follow us on Facebook
at https://www.facebook.com/ZeroBooks
and Twitter at https://twitter.com/Zer0Books